WELCOME

Submarines are the ultimate weapon of modern warfare and the most secret asset of any nation. Nuclear boats seek to dominate and control the subterranean 'battlespace' while diesel boats sit quietly in the shallow water where they often land special forces. New Air Independent Propulsion (AIP) technology allows modern diesel-electric submarines to stay under the ocean for much longer, boosting their capability to remain undetected.

NATO forces rarely comment about their submarine operations and as China and Russia invest in new boats, both the US and UK fleets are preparing for the future, commissioning new Virginia- and Astute-class attack boats

as well as Columbo and Dreadnought ballistic subs. Across Europe, only the UK and France field nuclear-powered boats. India has built its first ballistic submarine, while Brazil is in the process of procuring its first nuclear-powered submarine. Russia remains a powerful nuclear force and China is building a fleet to dominate the Pacific Rim. In 2021, Australia announced it plans to join the 'nuclear club' with an eight strong fleet – although its submarines will not carry nuclear weapons. Across the Far East and Middle East, most nations operate conventionally powered vessels.

The submarine is a versatile platform which can project military power, present a psychological threat to an adversary's surface fleet, support land-based covert operations and when required, deliver lethal force. The US Navy has nuclear ballistic submarines permanently deployed in the Atlantic and the Pacific ready as part of its deterrent policy, while the UK is known to have at least one ballistic vessel at sea armed with nuclear warheads. Moscow claims to have as many as five boats deployed at any one time.

The huge Typhoon- and Delta-class vessels face retirement, and Russia has proceeded

with plans to introduce a new Borei-class of submarines, the first of which was launched in 2007. The Borei submarines have been designed to carry the new Bulava missiles, which have a range of 8,000km. President Putin has also ordered the development of a new 'special operations' capable force which includes older submarines being converted to carry smaller submarines. But, while it is clear this new concept has experienced problems, the cost of the war in Ukraine has diverted money away from submarine development and stalled any progress with the new submarine force. China is seen as a major threat – poised to invade Taiwan and constantly claiming sovereignty of international waterways in the South China Sea. Submarines will be critical in future warfare. Their ability – especially nuclear-powered fleets – to operate worldwide in total secrecy is a powerful weapon.

David Reynolds Editor

CONTENTS

ISBN: 978 1 83632 029 6
Editor: David Reynolds
Senior editor, specials: Roger Mortimer
Email: roger.mortimer@keypublishing.com
Cover Design: Steve Donovan
Design: SJmagic DESIGN SERVICES, India
Advertising Sales Manager: Sam Clark
Email: sam.clark@keypublishing.com
Tel: 01780 755131
Advertising Production: Becky Antoniades
Email: Rebecca.antoniades@keypublishing.com

SUBSCRIPTION/MAIL ORDER
Key Publishing Ltd, PO Box 300,
Stamford, Lincs, PE9 1NA
Tel: 01780 480404
Subscriptions email:
subs@keypublishing.com

Mail Order email: orders@keypublishing.com
Website: www.keypublishing.com/shop

PUBLISHING
Group CEO and Publisher: Adrian Cox

Published by
Key Publishing Ltd, PO Box 100,
Stamford, Lincs. PE9 1XQ
Tel: 01780 755131
Website: www.keypublishing.com

PRINTING
Precision Colour Printing Ltd, Haldane,
Halesfield 1, Telford, Shropshire TF7 4QQ

DISTRIBUTION
Seymour Distribution Ltd, 2 Poultry Avenue,
London EC1A 9PU
Enquiries Line: 02074 294000

KEY Publishing

THE SILENT SERVICE

Since the introduction of the submarine, the 'silent service' as it is known, has remained at the forefront of naval warfare, providing surveillance, hunting enemy boats, and delivering lethal firepower. The ability of these vessels to hide and evade detection gives submarine commanders a psychological advantage over surface warships as well as the capability to strike with surprise. Referred to as 'boats', submarines operate in a world of darkness and secrecy. Every time they submerge on an operational patrol, they enter a realm of covert warfare that few people have an awareness of.

The submarine is the most powerful asset in modern warfare. Increasingly, nations see these silent leviathans of the deep as the ultimate military asset in a hi-tech world where satellites can track planes, ships and almost anything, apart from a submarine. These vessels can remain at sea for months without trace, with commanders sometimes hiding their war machines in a thermocline – the layer between the warmer water at the surface and the cooler deep water below.

The ability of these vessels to hide and evade detection gives submarines an advantage over surface warships and the capability of striking with surprise. (US DoD)

Killers of the Deep

The huge nuclear submarines that lurk in the dark waters of the ocean have earned a reputation as the 'killers of the deep', often celebrated in famous movies. *Das Boot* (1981) illustrated the shock and awe tactics of German U-boats in World War Two, while *The Hunt for Red October* (1990) depicted the terrifying might of Russian nuclear-powered ballistic boats.

The United Kingdom, France and the United States are the only countries within the NATO alliance that operate nuclear powered submarines. All three countries operate attack submarines, known as Sub-Surface Nuclear subs (SSNs) and Sub-Surface Ballistic subs (SSBNs). There is a major difference between the two types. The SSNs are armed with Tomahawk cruise missiles and torpedoes and patrol the channels around Europe, the North Atlantic and beyond. The Royal Navy (RN) operates Astute- and Trafalgar-class boats, with the Astute being the newer vessels. Occasionally one is seen on the surface off Norway or in Gibraltar but other than that, their movements are never revealed. SSNs can hunt and, if

Nations view these silent leviathans of the deep as the ultimate military asset in a hi-tech world where satellites can track planes, ships and almost anything — except a submarine. (UK MOD)

Each of the US Navy's 14 Ohio-class SSBNs carry submarine-launched ballistic missiles (SLBMs) with multiple warheads. (US DoD)

needed, attack enemy vessels, with much of their routine work being surveillance and the protection of surface warships. SSBNs are much bigger and carry the nuclear deterrent. They embark on extended secret patrols and are never seen until they surface again. It is understood that the three Alliance countries deploy their boats, which loiter on the seabed for months, poised for action. The 8,000-tonne Los Angeles-class represents the workhorse of the US Navy's SSN boats with almost 40 in commission. They deploy into the Atlantic, the Pacific, the Arctic and beyond. France operates the 2,600-tonne Rubis and the newer 5,300-tonne Suffern boats, armed with torpedoes and Exocet missiles.

All three nations deploy ballistic submarines, with the RN fielding the Vanguard-class SSBN, also known as the Trident submarine, because it carries the Trident D5 ballistic missile. These missiles can be fired at targets up to 4,000 miles away and are ejected from the sub's ballistic missile tubes by high-pressure gas which ignites when the weapon reaches the water surface.

The US Navy operates the 16,300-tonne Ohio-class to maintain its nuclear deterrent. Each of the 14 Ohio-class SSBNs originally carried up to 24 submarine-launched ballistic missiles (SLBMs) with multiple,

independently targeted warheads. However, under the provisions of the New Strategic Arms Reduction Treaty, each submarine has had four of its missile tubes permanently deactivated and now carries a maximum of 20 missiles. The Ohio-class design allows the submarines to operate for 15 or more years between major overhauls and on average, the boats deploy for 77 days at sea followed by 35 days in-port for maintenance.

France operates the 8,000-tonnes Triomphant-class SSBNs which carry the Mer-Sol Balistique Stratégique (MSBS) nuclear missile system. These SSBNs often sit in the remote black waters of the Arctic region – the High North – with their doomsday payloads at the ready. When these subs (known as bombers) leave port they never surface and only a handful of people onboard know where the vessel is heading.

Submarine Warfare

The first concepts of submerged operations that pioneered today's modern submarines emerged centuries ago, then leapt forward in development during World Wars One and Two. The British built a formidable force, but it was the Hitler's German Navy that adopted the ➲

The huge nuclear submarines that lurk in the dark waters of the ocean were portrayed on the big screen in films such as *Das Boot* and *The Hunt for Red October*. (US DoD)

hit and run tactic in the 1939-45 war. They used their U-boats to sink Allied shipping convoys in the Atlantic and were initially very successful, using so-called Wolf Packs of U-Boats which hunted and attacked supply ships. The allies quickly responded to the threat, building submarines that were widely deployed in the Atlantic, the Mediterranean and Pacific campaigns. The nuclear submarine forces of the US, the UK and France remained in the vanguard of operations in the post-war years.

The Cold War period of East-West political tension, which followed World War Two, saw US and UK submarines locked in cat and mouse chases with Soviet submarines in the waters of the High North. Lasting from 1947 to the fall of the Soviet Union in 1991, the Cold War placed a huge operational burden on British and American submarine forces who were constantly deployed on surveillance missions to find and track Soviet boats. Then, after the collapse of the Soviet Union, Moscow adopted a more open policy towards the West but still deployed submarines to harass Western fleets in European waters and in the Mediterranean – which they continue to do today. President Vladimir Putin directs his Northern Fleet to spy on the West in a dangerous sub-surface 'chase' which mirrors the Cold War activities.

In the past 50 years, governments have invested heavily in submarine design and their lethal capability, often deploying the submarine as a threat rather than a direct weapon. However, since 1945 there have been several incidents in which submarines have used their kinetic power. During the Indo-Pakistan war in December 1971, the Pakistani Daphné-class submarine PNS *Hangor* sank the Indian frigate INS *Khukri* with a homing torpedo. This was the heaviest loss that the Pakistani Navy inflicted on the Indian fleet during this war. After the attack on *Khukri*, the Indian Navy ceased its attacks on Karachi and moved the focus of its operations to East Pakistan ports such as Chittagong and Cox's Bazar (later part of Bangladesh). This was the first ship to be sunk by a submarine since World War Two.

Submarine attack warfare surfaced again in 1982, when Argentine forces invaded the British Falklands islands in the South Atlantic. The Argentines sent a conventionally powered boat to land special forces troops during the advance phase of their invasion. The RN quickly

The German Navy adopted hit and run attack tactics in World War Two. (German MoD)

In 1982 the Royal Navy quickly deployed six submarines, five nuclear-powered boats and a conventionally powered diesel sub, the Oberon-class vessel HMS *Onyx*, pictured. (UK MoD)

deployed six submarines, five nuclear-powered boats and a conventionally powered diesel sub – the Oberon-class vessel HMS *Onyx*, and the five nuclear boats HMS *Valiant*, (Valiant class), HMS *Spartan* and HMS *Splendid* (both Swiftsure class) and HMS *Conqueror* and HMS *Courageous* (both Churchill class). The British announced an exclusion zone around the Falklands and warned Argentina's President Leopoldo Galtieri and his administration that any shipping sent into this zone would be sunk. Within weeks, HMS *Conqueror* located the battleship ARA *General Belgrano* on April 30 and reported the sighting to London. The decision to attack *General Belgrano* was granted by Prime Minister Margaret Thatcher and her war cabinet on the morning of May 2. The speed of the order was aided by the interception of Argentine naval signals by British intelligence that indicated Buenos Aires was about to launch an imminent concerted naval and air attack on several fronts. The order to attack *General Belgrano* was relayed to Cdr Wreford-Brown in HMS *Conqueror*, and at shortly before 1500hrs local time, the nuclear-powered submarine fired three Mk 8 torpedoes at the cruiser – the newer Tigerfish guided torpedo she also carried was deemed less reliable in the circumstances. Two of the torpedoes struck *General Belgrano*, the first blowing off the ship's bows, the second striking her port side and causing an explosion which killed many of the victims of the sinking outright. It was the first time that a nuclear-powered submarine had fired weapons in an act of war. Such was the impact of the attack that Argentina's aircraft carrier and many of the fleet's main warships returned to port in fear of being attacked.

Submarines played a critical role during the Bosnian conflict when US and British submarines protected carrier operations in the Adriatic and in 1999 HMS *Splendid* became the first British submarine to fire Tomahawk ➲

The Cold War saw US and UK submarines locked in 'cat and mouse' chases with Soviet submarines, such as this Echo class, in the waters of the High North. (UK MoD)

In 1971 the Pakistani Daphné-class submarine PNS *Hangor*, similar to the one pictured, sank the Indian frigate INS *Khukri* with a homing torpedo. (Pakistan Navy)

The order to attack *General Belgrano* was relayed to Commander Christopher Wreford-Brown in HMS *Conqueror*. (UK MoD)

HMS *Valiant* took part in the Falklands War in 1982, arriving in the war zone on 17 May. She transmitted more than 300 early air-warning alerts and spent 101 days at sea. (UK MoD)

missiles in anger during NATO's air campaign against Yugoslavia. During the 11-week campaign the submarine launched an estimated 16 Tomahawk cruise missiles against Serb targets. In 2001, the British nuclear-powered submarines, HMS *Triumph*, and HMS *Trafalgar*, which at the time were deployed in the Arabian sea, fired Tomahawk cruise missiles into Al Qaeda training camps in Afghanistan. Later British nuclear-powered submarines fired missiles into Iraq during Operation Telic and in Libya during Operation Ellamy. Then in 2010, a North Korean two-man midget submarine sank the South Korean corvette ROKS *Cheonan* off Baengnyeong island.

Submerged Warfare

Today, submarines are home to highly trained personnel who can operate advanced weapons systems and remain undetected deep under the ocean. Submerged warfare was pioneered thousands of years ago in the siege of Syracuse in 413 BC when hollow sticks were used to breathe underwater and mount reconnaissance on enemy locations. The Greeks developed a diving bell which they successfully submerged, then in 1578 the English mathematician

During the 11-week Falklands campaign, HMS *Swiftsure* became the first British nuclear submarine to fire a Tomahawk in combat. (UK MoD)

Today submarines are home to highly trained personnel who can operate advanced weapons systems and remain undetected deep under the ocean. (US DoD)

William Bourne developed a prototype submarine with a cylindrical shape. It was fully enclosed and powered by underwater oars. By 1620 the Dutch inventor and engineer Cornelis Drebbel developed a submarine that could successfully submerge below the waves. King James I invited Drebbel to England where he continued his work with submarines. He made his subs out of rowing boats covered with watertight leather with oars that stuck out through watertight seals. Bladders were filled with water to allow a sub to descend and rise to the surface; the water was squeezed out and snorkel-like tubes brought in fresh air to inflate the bladders. Drebbel built three submarines in all. They were tested by the Royal Navy in the Thames in London. In one test, a sub stayed at a depth of about 15ft for three hours. King James and thousands of spectators watched the tests. However, despite its obvious capability, the Admiralty could not be persuaded to adopt the vessel for the fleet.

As the generations passed, France, Germany, America, and Russia all developed various forms of submersibles. These inventions were pushing submarine capability forward as engineers experimented with new technology. A French design based on an oval metal box equipped with a pump that delivered air was unveiled, while in America a small one-man submarine called the Turtle had been built. Then in the 1800s, the French built the Nautilus which

Crew live, work, eat and socialise together for weeks or months at a time in what is a small 'village' environment within the submarine. (US DoD)

included a sail to provide power when the boat was on the surface.

The South Americans joined the race to build a submarine and in 1837 produced the *Hipopótamo*, however it was later abandoned due to a lack of revenue to fund the project. Submarines played a small role during the American Civil War (1861-1865) when both sides used submerged vessels. The *Alligator* was deployed by the Union and the *Hunley* by Confederates. In 1863, a German engineer Julius H Kroehl designed a vessel called the Sub Marine Explorer which included a pressurised chamber to allow the crew to enter and exit underwater, that would later become known as the lock-out dive chamber. The sub was used for pearl diving off the coast of Panama. In the same year, the French Navy launched the Le Plongeur. It was revolutionary as it was the first submarine in the world to be operated by mechanised power. It was propelled by stored compressed air powering a reciprocating engine. The air was contained in 23 holding tanks and the system allowed the sub to move forward at a speed of 5nm. Compressed air was also used to empty the ballast tanks and allow the sub to surface. The submarine was armed with an electrically fired torpedo fixed to the end of a pole and a ram to break holes in enemy ships' hulls. It was primitive but effective at the time.

During the 1870s and 1880s, the design of the modern submarine began to emerge, through the inventions of the English clergyman and inventor George Garrett and Swede Thorsten Nordenfelt, who teamed up with the Irish engineer John Philip Holland. In 1878, Garrett built a 14ft-long, 4.5-ton vessel he named *Resurgam*. He then built a second and more famous vessel of the same name at Birkenhead, Merseyside, a year later. It weighed almost 30 tonnes and was 45ft long. The design included a wooden frame and iron plates, powered by a closed-cycle steam engine, but it was not regarded as practical. Nordenfelt then took the concept a step further and built a 56-tonne, 64ft-long submarine. It had a range of 150 miles and could carry a single torpedo. The vessel was sold to Russia, but it ran aground and was later abandoned.

The innovative Spanish engineer, Isaac Peral y Caballero, designed the world's first electric battery-powered submersible in 1888. The Peral submarine measured almost 72ft long, was about 10ft wide and could reach a speedy 3kts. A few years on, diesel-electric propulsion became the primary power system for the sub when submerged, while diesel engines were used on the surface to recharge the electric batteries. This new method of powering submarines was to have a major impact on 20th century maritime warfare. Irish engineer John Philip ➲

In 1878, George Garrett built a 14ft-long vessel which he named *Resurgam*. It weighed four tonnes. (Ed Pollock)

The innovative Spanish engineer Isaac Peral y Caballero designed the world's first electric battery-powered submersible in 1888. (Mde Vicente)

Holland now adopted electric power in his plans for the American military and sold his newest model, Holland VI, to the US Navy for $160,000. The 64-tonne submarine was commissioned into service as USS *Holland* in 1897.

Holland later introduced a new method of propulsion using a petrol engine. This turned a propeller while the boat cruised on the surface and supported a generator that produced electricity to charge the batteries necessary to run an electric motor during submerged operations. But petrol was highly flammable and unstable, while the batteries that ran the electric motor when the boat was submerged were heavy and potentially explosive. Finding a safer means of propulsion was needed if the submarine was ever to be submerged for long periods. Around the same time that Holland was creating his

submarines, German scientist Rudolf Diesel developed an excellent substitute for the petrol engine. Diesel's engine used a fuel that was more stable and could be stored safely. Plus, it did not need an electric spark to ignite the fuel, adding another element of safety. These advantages, plus improved fuel economy, granted submarines with diesel engines longer and safer cruises on the surface. While underwater, batteries were still necessary to provide power. Diesel engines were seen as the future and the US Navy soon followed the French practice, adopting the alternative engine in the early 1900s. Holland now started to market the design rights to his submarine and the RN ordered a batch of five vessels. Completed in 1901, the first vessel dived for the first time in April 1902 and was based at Portsmouth, as part of the First Submarine Flotilla. An early

Holland 1 was the first in a five-boat batch of Holland-class submarines ordered for the Royal Navy. She was lost in 1913 while under tow. (UK MoD)

Irish engineer John Philip Holland adopted electric power in his plans for the American military and sold the *Holland VI* to the US Navy. The 64-ton submarine was commissioned into service as USS *Holland* in 1897. (US DoD)

submarine snorkel was designed in 1916 by James Richardson, an assistant manager at a shipbuilding company in Greenock, Scotland. This allowed the submarine to avoid surfacing and was a significant tactical advantage.

World War One

Britain's blockade across the North Sea and the English Channel cut the flow of war supplies, food, and fuel to Germany during World War One. Germany retaliated by using its U-boat

U-boats prowled the Atlantic hunting allied shipping. They were Germany's only weapon of advantage as Britain had effectively blocked German ports to supplies. (German MoD)

A German U-Boat commander. Nazi submarines operated in 'wolf packs' attacking merchant ships and passenger vessels. (German MoD)

Faced with the possibility that Washington would enter the war over the incident, Germany ordered its U-boat fleet to spare passenger vessels. The order, however, was temporary. Germany built new and larger U-boats to punch holes in the British blockade, which was threatening to starve their country out of the war. In 1914, Germany had just 20 U-boats. By 1917, it had 140 and the U-boats had destroyed about a third of the world's merchant ships.

Life on board a submarine was difficult. Below the casing deck (the submarine's outer hull), there was little room, no spare water for washing and often the smell of fuel oil was thick in the air. The men who served in submarines were part of a close-knit community. They stood separate from the men who sailed in the surface fleet, who submariners referred to as 'skimmers'. Many rarely took all their clothes off during a three or four-week patrol and the shortage of space meant that sleeping accommodation was shared, one bunk space between two – while one sailor slept ➲

submarines to prowl the Atlantic, destroying neutral ships that were supplying the Allies. They were Germany's only weapon of advantage as Britain had effectively blocked German ports to supplies. The goal was to starve Britain before the British blockade defeated Germany. The U-boat fleet made its first strike on September 5, 1914, with an attack on a British light cruiser off the coast of Scotland, killing more than 200 crew. Two weeks later, another U-boat sank three British battle cruisers in a day, with the loss of nearly 900 men. Despite these successes, the Germans lost more U-boats than they sank during the early months of the war. Then, in February 1915, Germany announced that any vessel spotted off the UK coastline would be considered a legitimate target. U-boats attacked food and oil supplies bound for the British Isles as well as passenger ships. On May 7, 1915, a U-boat torpedoed the SS *Lusitania*, a Cunard passenger liner, off the coast of Ireland. Nearly 1,200 men, women, and children, including 128 Americans, lost their lives. The Allies and Americans considered the sinking an act of indiscriminate warfare.

The Atlantic convoys delivered war equipment from the United States to Britain and were seen as easy pickings for U-Boat crews. (UK MoD)

A German U Boat crew on the surface. The Germans deployed submarines in both world wars having established a powerful force in World War One which they used to attacks convoys. (German MoD)

On May 7, 1915, a U-boat torpedoed the SS *Lusitania*, a Cunard passenger liner, off the coast of Ireland. Nearly 1,200 men, women and children died. (US DoD)

another worked. Food was stored wherever room could be found. The diesel engines generated heat throughout the boat and the air quality was often very poor. In order not to be spotted, submarines were under strict orders to only surface at night. Depending on the sea state, hatches were opened to allow fresh air to vent through the submarine.

New submarine designs were developed during the final years of World War One – the most notable being what some naval officers called the 'unhinged idea' to create submarine aircraft carriers. These subs were equipped with a steam catapult to launch small seaplanes. This Admiralty's plan was to use the submarine as a forward reconnaissance platform ahead of the fleet, an essential capability at the time as radar was not available. The first RN carrier submarine was HMS *M2*, but she sank in a tragic accident and the concept of deploying seaplanes on submarines was abandoned.

World War Two

By 1939 submarines were bigger and faster and had been fitted with what was then regarded as sophisticated detection technology and echo sounders. During World War Two, RN submarines deployed around the world with submarines serving in the Home Fleet based around the UK, at Alexandria in Egypt with the Mediterranean Fleet, as well as the Far East. At the opening of the war Germany

had 57 submarines under the command of Commodore Karl Dönitz, who had served on U-boats in World War One. He believed the war would be decided in the Atlantic and that he could cripple the Allies with a force of 300 U-boats. In May 1940, German dictator Adolf Hitler approved unrestricted submarine warfare on all shipping around the UK. British Prime Minister Winston Churchill coined the phrase 'Battle of the Atlantic' on March 6, 1941, deliberately echoing the Battle of Britain to emphasise its importance.

Although the British implemented a convoy system at the start of the war, it was poorly protected and heavily attacked in the first 18 months. Radar remained primitive and aircraft were few in number, lacked sufficient range and could not provide escort coverage at night. Thankfully, the British were able to break the German cipher messages and develop improvements in radar technology, while the effectiveness of attacks by long-range RAF bombers and escort carriers led to the sinking of 41 U-boats in May 1943, including eight in one day. This success cut the volume of attacks, but the U-boats returned to the British coast in 1944 after the development of snorkel ventilation tubes allowed them to operate longer and deeper underwater to reduce the chance of detection by radar and enemy aircraft. However, they suffered heavy

The British diesel-powered submarine HMS *Ultimatum*. Space on these vessels was very limited for the crew and fresh food soon ran out. (UK MoD)

losses and few successes. Following Hitler's suicide on April 30, 1945, Dönitz served as his successor and ordered Nazi forces to cease operations and surrender. The 45 U-boats at sea surfaced and proceeded to ports designated by the Allies. Germany lost almost

The British Royal Navy developed submarine aircraft carriers equipped with a steam catapult to launch small seaplanes. (UK MoD)

HMS *Ursula* returns home to port in April 1984. The commander had sailed 'blind' for six days and nights after the sub was rammed and the periscope smashed. The Jolly Roger is flown in respect of their success against the Germans. (UK MoD)

British submarines operating in the Mediterranean often called in at Malta for food and fuel. (UK MoD)

The American Balao-class submarine USS *Sablefish*, which entered service after World War Two. (US DoD)

three-quarters of the U-boats it built during this war despite them being highly successful against Allied shipping over the course of both wars.

At the outbreak of hostilities with Japan on December 7, 1941, the United States began building submarines at a rapid pace. In the Pacific, they wanted large boats that could run fast then surface to attack shore-based targets with their deck guns. These boats needed to carry as many as 20 torpedoes, deploy mines and carry fuel and food to last up to 100 days at sea. The US Navy fleet included many that had been built in 1939 with a flat casing deck, and surface armament in the form of several anti-aircraft machine guns and a larger deck gun for use against surface vessels. The batteries of these older submarines did not store enough electricity to allow them to stay submerged for very long and so they spent most of the time on the surface. They were designed for a patrol endurance of eight weeks.

The American submarines were based on three separate types: the Gato, Balao, and later the Tench. They were around 300ft long with a beam (width) of 27ft. Both the Gato and

Balao class were heavily armed with torpedo tubes; six forward, four aft. They were also armed with more conventional weapons. The Balao-class was armed with a forward-facing 5in deck gun and four machine guns. US Navy submarines recorded their greatest successes against Japanese merchant vessels and warships. In all, US Navy submarines destroyed 1,314 enemy warships in the Pacific, representing 55%

of all Axis power warships lost and a total of 5.3 million tonnes of shipping.

After World War Two, huge advances were made in submarine design. Today, nuclear power has enabled countries such as Russia, the US, UK, India, and France to operate a new generation of boats that if required to do so, can remain at sea for several years without the need to be refuelled. ●

Russia deploys subs into the High North and once at sea, these boats remain submerged for weeks or months at a time in the deep waters of the Atlantic. (Russian MoD)

THE ENEMY BELOW

Submarines are a strategic asset, armed with a deadly arsenal and capable of delivering covert operations that are often unknown and rarely revealed to the public. In the 21st century the submarine is the most potent weapon of modern warfare.

Once at sea submarines submerge for weeks or months. The crew operate within their own community, living, working, and eating side by side. Understanding and being considerate of fellow workmates is a must in such a tight-knit environment. Ironing boards are rarely used

but if required, they can be found strapped behind the toilet doors. The only privacy in bed is a small curtain, and everything 'galley' – the kitchen – is designed so as not to fall with special facilities to avoid hot water spills. The air is cleaned and recycled, however, if someone gets a cold it is likely the entire crew will catch it. British submariners are often allowed to wear trainers at sea as it can help reduce noise and, in some situations, the commander can give permission for personnel to wear sports kit as it can help boost morale. Food is a major part of the daily routine, with steak, fish and chips, and

roast dinner all appearing in a menu that rotates every seven days.

Due to their sensitive operational deployments, the Ministry of Defence never discusses where Royal Navy (RN) submarines operate, as it would compromise the secret nature of their work. From the darkness of deep water anywhere across the globe, the Sub Surface Ballistic Nuclear (SSBNs) vessels can loiter with their nuclear weapons ready to deploy, while the Sub Surface Nuclear (SSN) boats can stalk enemy subs, mount coastal surveillance, and launch cruise

Moscow still operates several upgraded Oscar- and Delta-class submarines. (Russian MoD)

missiles. In addition, both nuclear powered and conventionally powered boats can transit special forces to their objective. Big and black, these huge vessels can sit on the seabed and hide in the ocean's trenches.

The ability to evade detection and outwit an adversary by employing tactical awareness was most relevant during the Cold War. During this period of geopolitical tension US and UK nuclear submarines attempted to own the waters of the North Atlantic and Norwegian Sea, as well as the North Sea, with the aim of preventing the other from operating in territorial waters. American and British submarines worked together to identify and chase Soviets away from the UK and the US east coast. The Soviet submarines included the Yankee-class, Project 667A Navaga, as well as the Delta class and Typhoon ballistic boats. Their SSNs included the Sierra class and Charlie class, and they could also deploy a fleet of diesel-electric boats. The US Navy's ballistic submarines included the George Washington-class and more than 12 different classes of SSN. The British deployed the Polaris submarines of the Resolution-class as well as Churchill, Swiftsure, Trafalgar and Valiant-class hunter-killer subs.

Life below the surface

Since the development of the first military submarines, space on board has been an issue. The galley, the heads (toilet) and accommodation areas are designed to be as compact as possible. Everything on a submarine has its place and everything is secured. During World War Two, crewmen rarely took off their uniforms due to the lack of water and washing facilities. Most grew beards and when the men emerged from their boats after a patrol, they usually smelt of diesel and smoke. In the post-war years of diesel-electric submarines, washing facilities continued to ➲

Modern submarines are strategic assets armed with a deadly arsenal and capable of delivering covert operations. (UK MoD)

During the Cold War the enemy below the surface included huge Russian Delta-class ballistic class submarines. (Russian MoD)

A meal served with minced beef is known as a 'Jack Roast', while a knife and fork are 'fighting irons', and the food waste disposal unit called 'Peter the Eater'. Finally, any sort of drink is called a 'wet' and passing it to your mate to finish is termed 'sandy bottoms'.

While submariners' slang remains in use today, the shape and design of submarines across the generation has changed dramatically. New nuclear-powered hunter-killer and ballistic boats carry smaller crews and more weapons – and they have the capability to stay at sea for longer. The bigger ballistic-carrying missiles submarines provide more space, allowing the crew to enjoy a small gym and most individuals have their own bed. But of course, there is no sunlight, no natural oxygen, and no social media. The submarine must remain undetected and while it is covered in acoustic shells, noise inside the boat must also be kept to a minimum. The crew breathe oxygen that is created onboard by a recycling machine and submariners take Vitamin D tablets to make up for the lack of sunlight. Most crews include a team of several chefs who cook four meals a day with varying menus. Carrying food stores for up to 150 days, the chefs may have just two ovens, a range plate, and a fryer.

Personnel can elect to receive two messages a week from home. These 60-word notes are known as FamilyGrams and are received via a

be restricted, living conditions were spartan with personnel forced to share bunks, with one man on watch and the other sleeping. Crews often spoke of the race to breathe in the fresh air when the submarine surfaced, and the main hatch was opened. To save water, the crew would often use a very small amount to clean their teeth and then wash – this became known as a 'submariners' bird bath'.

In the post war years submariners developed a unique language code. A mate or colleague is an 'oppo'. A Naval policeman is known as the regulator and is sometimes called 'the crusher'. Nightmares experienced by crewmen on long patrols are referred to as 'coffin dreams'. The 'donkshop' is the name given to the engine room, torpedoes are known as 'fish'. The senior rates' accommodation is called 'the goat shed'.

Royal Navy Trafalgar-class Sub Surface Nuclear (SSN) were, until recently, the mainstay of the hunter-killer force – they have largely been replaced by the Astute class. (UK Mod)

A Royal Navy Resolution-class submarine which carried the UK's Polaris nuclear deterrent during the Cold War. (UK MoD)

special communications cable towed behind the sub – but crew members cannot reply.

The 150m-long boats – the bombers – can be at sea for months. Their patrols are so secret that no-one ever knows exactly how long they will be away for or where they operate. There's a rest area where crew members can relax, watch films, and eat – one for junior rates, one for senior rates (non-commissioned officers) and a wardroom for officers. US Navy submarines are regarded as the most comfortable and best equipped, with hi-tech catering and recreation facilities. The Control Room is the command centre of the boat. It houses the steering position, the periscopes and the navigation plotting table. It also houses the tactical systems department, which uses data provided by the sound room and other sensors to ensure safe travel in peacetime and to provide target information during wartime. Submarines are normally 'rigged for red' to allow the use of the periscope at night, dusk, and dawn without interference from bright light in the control room.

The High North

In the vast waters of the High North submarines stalk each other at close quarters in the ocean's blackwaters using sonar, radar, and other sensors, which allow a submarine commander to obtain a near 360° picture of the sea around his boat. Crew members can simultaneously track multiple objects above and below the surface. These objects may be friendly or hostile ships and submarines, but also underwater rocks or shoals of fish. These challenging situations are often described as 'warfare with your eyes shut' and for those ➲

Ballistic submarines from Britain, France and the United States were at high readiness during the Cold War. (NATO)

involved, it can be intense, sometimes terrifying, and constantly stressful. During the Cold War period, submariners in the Royal Navy and US Navy were effectively operating on a war footing, in an environment where psychological pressure was immense and the risk of collision constant as subs shadowed each other.

In the depths of the sea, out of sight of politicians and the public, Moscow and the West set about a pseudo war from 1947 to 1991. There were numerous serious incidents in which Royal Navy submarines returned to port showing visible damage from suspected collisions with Soviet boats. The most serious included the clash of HMS *Warspite*, a 4,500 tonne Valiant-class nuclear submarine, with an unknown Soviet submarine in 1968, which rolled Warspite over to 65° and traumatised members of the crew. Then in 1981, HMS *Sceptre*, a Swiftsure-class boat, sustained severe damage in an impact that ripped away part of her forward casing deck and part of the fin.

Crew on board a Royal Navy nuclear submarine in the 1970s. Note the submariner in the background is smoking, a practice that has since been banned. (UK MoD)

This image shows the limited space in the galley area aboard a Dutch submarine in the 1980s. (Dutch MoD)

On April 10, 1963, the USS *Thresher* sank during deep-diving tests east of Cape Cod, Massachusetts, with the loss of 129 crew and shipyard personnel aboard. There was no suggestion of Soviet involvement. Then in May 1968, the USS *Scorpion*, a 3,000-tonne Skipjack-class nuclear-powered submarine, which operated widely during the Cold War, was lost at sea and claims quicky surfaced that the Soviets were responsible. The boat had been tasked to monitor a Soviet Echo-class submarine near the Azores, which was operating with a task force of warships. *Scorpion*'s Commander Francis Slattery had reported that he was closing on the Soviet submarine and research group at a depth of 350ft to begin surveillance. That was the last message received from the sub and on May 20, 1968, it was reported missing. A major search

An officer, wearing the traditional submariner's white jersey, aboard the nuclear-powered Trafalgar-class submarine HMS *Trenchan*. (DPL)

The Royal Navy submariner's qualification badge, the Dolphins, worn by all British submariners on their dress uniforms. (DPL)

An officer aboard a nuclear-powered submarine views surface contacts via the periscope. (UK MoD)

to periscope depth. A later theory was that a fire in the torpedo room had caused a torpedo to explode in the tube. There were many other theories included in Ed Offley's book *Scorpion Down* which suggested that *Scorpion* was sunk by a Soviet submarine during a standoff. In the same year, the Soviet submarine K-129 was mysteriously lost in the Pacific, the French submarine *Minerve* went down in the Mediterranean and the Israeli boat INS *Dakar* was lost off Crete.

The danger of identifying the exact location of another submarine was highlighted in 1992, when an American attack boat was hit by the Russian Navy nuclear submarine B-276 *Kostroma* off Severomorsk, on the Russian coast. The latter was sat under the US Navy vessel and then suddenly surfaced, apparently unaware that it was about to crash into the USS *Baton Rouge*. It was one of the last known sub-on-sub accidents and took place on February 11, 1992, not long after the Soviet Union collapsed in December 1991, when it appeared on paper that the former USSR offered little military threat. The US Navy had been monitoring all Soviet submarine movements during the Cold War. And despite the demise of the powerful communist state, the Pentagon still wanted to shadow the Northern Fleet, especially around the Murmansk naval region, home to the main submarine force operating in the Atlantic. The US 6,900-tonne nuclear-powered Los Angeles-class attack submarine USS *Baton Rouge* was operating off the northern coast of Russia in international waters,

was launched and in October 1968 sections of the hull were located 400 miles southwest of the Azores sat at a depth of 9,800ft. An official US Navy inquiry board stated that a catastrophic incident onboard the submarine had taken place. Retired US Admiral Dave Oliver, who served in both diesel boats and nuclear submarines, supported this conclusion. He wrote in his book *Against the Tide* that *Scorpion* was lost because of hydrogen build-up due to changes in the ventilation line while proceeding

and was believed to be loitering approximately 16 miles off Kildin island in the Barents Sea where Soviet forces had based a long-range missile regiment.

The *Baton Rouge* was presumed to be on a highly secret mission and was unaware that a 7,200-tonne Soviet sub was lurking beneath them. The *Kostroma*, a Sierra-class, was launched in 1984 with the *Carp, Kostroma, Nizhniy Novgorod,* and *Pskov* later entering service, and all operating

The contested waters of the High North are regularly visited by Russian and NATO submarines. This ice block which this US Navy sub has broken through appears to be at least 2ft thick. (US DoD)

Luis dived to the seabed while on the ... HMS *Brilliant* remained undamaged. ... ng of the Belgrano by HMS *Conqueror* ... psychological fear on the Argentine ... group who ordered the surface fleet to ... coastal waters, leaving the San *Luis* ... A week later the RN were hunting

Map showing the waters of the High North.

Arctic Ocean

GREENLAND

Franz Josef Land
(Russia)

Svalbard
(Norway)

Greenland
Sea

Novaya
Zemlya

Jan Mayen

Barents
Sea

Kara
Sea

Bear Island

Norwegian
Sea

Murmansk

North
Sea

SWEDEN

White
Sea

Archangel'sk

FINLAND

NORWAY

RUSSIA

Baltic
Sea

St. Petersburg

ESTONIA

NORTH

DENMARK

LATVIA

0   200   400   600   800

LITHUANIA

Moscow

Kilometres

GERMANY   POLAND

The US Navy's *Baton Rouge* was presumed to be on a highly secret covert mission and was unaware that a 7,200 tonne Soviet sub sat beneath them. (US DoD)

the *San Luis* and the Argentine commander reported to Buenos Aires that he had been fired upon by a RN submarine which he evaded. In late May, the *San Luis* detected the Type 21 anti-submarine frigates HMS *Arrow* and HMS *Alacrity* in Falkland Sound. Masked by the noise produced by the fast-moving frigates, the *San Luis* allegedly moved within 5km of the *Alacrity*, fired another SST-4 torpedo and readied a second for launch. Yet again the wires of the SST-4 cut out shortly after launch. Captain Azcueta reported his concerns and headed back to the mainland in frustration to have the system repaired. But before repairs could be completed, the Argentine garrison surrendered on June 14, 1982. Many observers suggest that had the Argentine submarine force been at high readiness and well trained, it would have posed a real threat to the Royal Navy Task Force. Instead, it posed a nuisance factor and achieved very little, with *Santa Fe* being removed from the operation within days and the *San Luis* almost incapable of any operational effectiveness.

Secret Mission

Just two months after the Falklands conflict, HMS *Conqueror* was deployed on another

[t]he Argentine Navy only had one [opera]tional submarine left – ARA *San Luis*. [It offe]red the capability to deliver both 'threat [and s]trike' against the RN. The German-built [Type] 209 diesel-powered submarine, which [had b]een purchased in the early 1970s had [been] assigned the pennant number S-32. It [enter]ed service in 1974 with the Argentine [navy] and was intended to be the first of several [purch]ases, but a lack of funds prevented a [large] procurement and only one more was [order]ed. The 1,295-tonne submarine had a [crew] of just 31 and its German engineering was [highly] regarded. The sub was quiet, small, and [potent]ially deadly. But in 1982, the problem [for the] Argentine fleet was that many of its [trained] crew and officers were in Germany [under]going additional training.

[On] April 3, the ARA *San Luis*, which had [been h]eld back in Argentina received orders to [join] the Falklands. The boat carried a batch [of M]ark-37 anti-sub torpedoes and ten [SST-4] wire-guided anti-ship torpedoes. The [San Lu]is's highly efficient systems allowed it to [dive] 1,000ft, but it was in poor condition – [a requir]ed maintenance period had not

The Russian boat that collided with the *Baton Rouge* is widely suspected to have been the *Kostroma* (B276), a Sierra Class launched in 1984. (US DoD)

top-secret mission in the Barents Sea. The submarine was ordered to acquire a Soviet passive sonar array from a Polish-flagged towing vessel. At the time both the UK and the US sought more information on a highly sensitive Russian towed array system. This was attached to a submarine or a surface ship on a long cable to keep the array's sensors away from the vessel allowing quiet, low noise emitting threats to be magnified. The operation, a joint mission between British and American forces, was conducted on the boundary of Soviet territorial waters. *Conqueror* had been outfitted with an unusual set of tools: a pair of remote-controlled heavy steel cutting blades and television cameras, all in the interest of stealing a top secret Russian towed sonar array.

There are two types of sonar: active and passive. Active sonar broadcasts short bursts of sound, known as pings, that travel through the ocean before bouncing back towards the ship that made them. Passive sonar simply picks up noise in the ocean, listening for

Royal Navy hunter-killer class submarines which deployed to the South Atlantic in 1982 sent a wave of fear through the Argentine fleet after the *General Belgrano* was sunk. (DPL)

suspicious sounds such as active sonar pings and machinery noise. Passive sonar can be difficult to use effectively, since the ship doing the listening often has to contend with its own noise, particularly the sound its propellers make churning through the water. As a result, passive sonars are often towed a mile or more behind a ship, something the Soviets had been doing since 1980. The device emitted no noise itself and virtually nothing could be learned about the array without sitting in front of one and taking it apart, which is why the US and UK forged a plan to recover a system. The plan, never officially revealed by the UK Ministry of Defence, was to approach the ship towing the array, a Polish intelligence vessel, and cut the device loose. HMS *Conqueror* completed the task, and the device was recovered to the UK before being sent to the US for analysis. ●

The crippled Argentine submarine Santa Fé was towed out of Gryvitken, South Georgia, and sunk. (DPL)

GLOBAL SUBMARINE CAPABILITY

S ubmarines provide global ability; they project political intent, military force and can influence an adversary's decision making with reports of their presence in an area. These monsters of the deep can, when required, launch cruise-missiles or, in a worst-case scenario, a 'doomsday' strike of nuclear warheads against an enemy.

The US Navy pioneered nuclear-powered submarines, with USS *Nautilus* being the first boat to be commissioned into the fleet in 1955. The then Soviet Union, the UK and France followed but it was almost 20 years before China launched its first nuclear-powered submarine, the *Changzheng,* in 1974. In the past decade Beijing has invested heavily in its sub-surface force, with six attack submarines and six ballistic boats in service. In 2016, the Indian Navy commissioned its first nuclear-powered submarine into service, INS *Arihant*, and is building three more. These six nations dominate the 'nuclear submarine club', but others are preparing to join. Brazil entered a strategic partnership with France in 2008 to build its first nuclear submarine, *Álvaro Alberto*, which is due to enter service in 2032. In a project between the US, Britain, and the Australian government, known as AUKUS, the Canberra administration is investing millions of dollars to ensure that it can operate nuclear powered submarines in the Pacific – although the boats will not carry nuclear weapons.

Nuclear-powered submarines are increasingly preferred to conventionally powered submarines. They do not need to be refuelled and can stay submerged for extended periods of time, allowing commanders to stay deployed for longer – the only reason they need to return to port is to restock food supplies.

Submarines provide global ability; they project political intent, military force and can influence an adversary's decision making with reports of their presence in an area. (UK MoD)

The Soviet Union followed the US nuclear development and built their own submarines a few years after the USS *Nautilus* entered service. (US DoD)

The US has dominated the world of nuclear submarines since they first built the *Nautilus*. (US DoD)

Submarine Strike

In the past two decades the Royal Navy (RN) and the US have sent submarines into action several times against terrorist and state actors. In 2001, a RN Trafalgar-class nuclear attack submarine took part in a cruise missile strike on Al-Qaeda and Taliban forces in Afghanistan during Operation Veritas. The action came after the attacks of September 11, 2001, and destroyed the terrorist organisations' training bases. The weapons were launched from a secret location deep below the surface. Then in April 2003, during the invasion of Iraq, the submarine HMS *Turbulent* launched 30 Tomahawk cruise missiles prior to the Coalition land invasion. When the sub returned to the UK, she flew the Jolly Roger flag to denote the fact that she had been in operational action. As part of the UK military's 2011 intervention in Libya, the Trafalgar-class submarine, HMS *Triumph* fired her Tomahawk cruise missiles on three occasions: first on March 19, then again on March 20, and finally on March 24. Her primary targets were Libyan air-defence installations around the city of Sabha. HMS

Triumph then returned to the UK on April 3, 2011, flying a Jolly Roger adorned with six small Tomahawk axes to indicate the missiles fired in the operation.

In 1993, HMS *Triumph* sailed to Australia, covering 41,000 miles while submerged and without any forward support. This remains the longest solo deployment by any British nuclear submarine.

The US submarine service saw action in 1991, when on day three of the Gulf War, the fast attack submarines USS *Louisville* and USS *Pittsburgh* fired the first submarine-launched Tomahawk cruise missiles in combat history. Then in 1996 the USS *Jefferson* fired 17

Tomahawks against Saddam Hussein's forces which were attacking villages in Kurdistan, during Operation Desert Strike. In August 1998, the fast attack submarine USS *Columbia* fired 73 Tomahawks at the Zhawar Kili al-Badr terrorist training and support complex, 30 miles southwest of Khowst, Afghanistan. The mission, codenamed Operation Infinite Reach, was in retaliation to the twin al-Qaeda attacks on the embassies in East Africa on August 7. After the attacks on the US in 2001, submarine-launched Tomahawks were directed into Afghanistan by American attack subs that were also in the forefront of action against Iraq in the 2003 invasion – again launching cruise ➲

China took almost two decades to join the 'nuclear submarine club'. (PLAN)

missile strikes. During the conflict in Libya in 2011 the fast attack submarines USS *Providence* (SSN 719) and USS *Scranton* (SSN 756) fired Tomahawk missiles at strategic targets as part of a Coalition operation. More recently, in April 2018, a US attack submarine launched Tomahawk missiles at military targets in Syria after Bashar al-Assad's government directed poison gas against its own people. As part of the co-ordinated air and missile strike, Tomahawk land attack missiles were launched from the guided missile cruiser USS *Monterey*, the destroyer USS *Laboon* and USS *Higgins,* as well as the fast attack submarine USS *John Warner*.

Submarine Power

The US Navy continues to field the most powerful nuclear submarine fleet and while Russia claims to operate more subs, many require repair and maintenance in a fleet with little operational experience. The US Navy's Los Angeles-class submarines, built between 1972 and 1996, have formed the backbone of the American Navy's SSN (attack) fleet, with 34 having seen service. The nuclear-powered Los Angeles-subs carry Tomahawk land-attack cruise missiles (LACMs) and MK-48 torpedoes. The boats were primarily developed for anti-submarine warfare but are also capable of inserting Special Forces and laying mines. As a result of technical improvements over time, there are three variants of the Los Angeles-class. Beginning with the USS *Providence* in 1984, the vessels were equipped with 12 vertical launch tubes for Tomahawk missiles to complement the original Los Angeles class's four torpedo tubes.

The USS *San Juan*, commissioned in 1988, was the first of the 'improved' quieter Los Angeles-class submarines, fitted with an advanced sonar system, and capable of operating under ice. According to the Pentagon, a total of 27 of the Los Angeles-class submarines will be retired by the mid-2030s, and five will be refuelled to extend their lifespan.

The Seawolf-class SSN was intended to be the replacement for the Los Angeles but

Technology used to build British and American nuclear-powered submarines will be used in the new AUKUS contract with Australia. (DPL)

A French Rubis-class nuclear-powered submarine – Paris commissioned its first nuclear boat in 1971. (French MoD)

In 2001, a Royal Navy Trafalgar-class nuclear attack submarine took part in a cruise missile strike on Al-Qaeda and Taliban forces in Afghanistan during Operation Veritas. (UK MoD)

The impact of a Tomahawk cruise missile detonation. (UK MoD)

the combination of the end of the Cold War, the reduced the operational requirement and soaring build costs resulted in cutbacks and only three were built: USS *Seawolf*, USS *Connecticut*, and USS *Jimmy Carter*. Based at Bangor Trident Base in Washington State, the Seawolfs were originally developed to hunt the Soviet ballistic SSBNs, the Seawolf attack submarine running significantly faster and quieter than the Los Angeles class. The boat's stealth capabilities also make it well suited for the insertion of units such as Navy SEALs. Although it does not possess a vertical launch capability, it can fire Tomahawk missiles through its torpedo tubes. The Seawolf-class submarines are larger than the Los Angeles-class submarines; they also carry more weapons and have twice as many torpedo tubes. The boats can handle up to 50 UGM-109 Tomahawk 50 cruise missiles for attacking land and sea surface targets. The boats also have extensive equipment to support shallow water operations. The USS *Jimmy Carter* is roughly 100ft longer than the other two boats

of her class, due to the insertion of a section known as the Multi-Mission Platform (MMP) which allows launch and recovery of remotely operated underwater vehicles and special operations forces.

The Virginia class, designed by the Electric Boat Corporation of Connecticut, is the next generation of US nuclear attack submarines and has been developed as a more cost-effective alternative to the Seawolf class. With 22 vessels already in service, the Virginia-class will eventually fully replace the Los Angeles on operations. The submarine's ability to operate effectively in littoral waters, primarily

due to its 'fly-by-wire' control system, gives it an advantage over the Los Angeles class, while its unmanned undersea vehicles (UUV) and special force delivery vehicles make it suitable for intelligence gathering and special operation forces missions. Furthermore, unlike the Seawolf class, the Virginia class possesses vertical launch tubes for firing its land-attack Tomahawk missiles. In future, 12 slightly larger Columbia SSBNs will replace the Ohio class, and these are due into service in 2031. They will never need to be refuelled throughout their life. They have been developed in collaboration with the UK, which will deploy the sub under the name of the Dreadnought-class SSBNs, replacing the current Vanguard class. The UK operates four Vanguard (SSBN) submarines and is building a seven-strong fleet of Astute-class SSNs – it currently retains one Trafalgar-class hunter-killer boat in service.

In 2024 the Russian Navy listed 73 boats in its fleet, with the US maintaining 72 and China 69. But despite Moscow topping the table, many of their nuclear boats are not regarded as 'operationally capable' due to age and lack of maintenance.

Post Cold War

After the Cold War, the lack of repair and overhaul was listed as a major factor in several accidents. In the worst tragedy, on August 12, 2000, the Russian nuclear-powered submarine *Kursk* sank during naval exercises of the

The Royal Navy operate the Trident D5 and the Tomahawk cruise missile. (UK MoD)

Raising the US flag is among the first duties carried out by the crew when a US attack submarine surfaces. (US DoD)

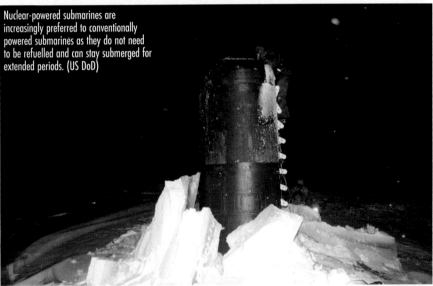

Nuclear-powered submarines are increasingly preferred to conventionally powered submarines as they do not need to be refuelled and can stay submerged for extended periods. (US DoD)

Northern Fleet in the Barents Sea, inside the Arctic Circle. The entire 118-strong crew were lost aboard the Oscar II-class submarine which had only been built six years previously in 1994. According to the Russian navy, it had not been carrying nuclear warheads so there was never a danger of radiation leaks. A desperate Russian rescue operation took place in which other countries, including Britain, offered their assistance. The Russians failed to establish radio communication with the stricken vessel and repeated failed efforts of mini submarines sent to open the hatch cost valuable hours. The rescue operation was hampered by icy waters, stormy weather, and poor underwater visibility, but the Russians were also slow to arrive at the scene. It was claimed that some of the submarine's crew might have been rescued had the response been quicker as the *Kursk sank* to the seafloor at 350ft, a relatively short distance from the surface. An official investigation determined that the failure of one of *Kursk*'s hydrogen peroxide-fuelled torpedoes triggered an explosion. The disaster sparked intense public criticism of the government and the Navy and left a stain on President Vladimir Putin's first term in office.

In 2008, 20 Russian submariners died when a Halon fire suppressant was accidently ignited aboard the *Nerpa*, an Akula-class nuclear submarine. The Halon gas was released inside two compartments of the submerged submarine during the vessel's sea trials in the Sea of Japan, asphyxiating the victims.

In 2010 the Russian Navy developed a vessel for future seabed warfare. The Belgorod project involved the transformation of a former Oscar II that enabled her to act as the mothership to a spy submarine. At the same time, the *Podmoskovye*, a former Delta IV class SSBN was converted as part of the project. Then in 2019 the Belgorod-modified Oscar II and the world's longest submarine (a special mission platform deployed with the Losharik spy submarine

A US Navy attack submarine surfaces at speed during a drill. (US DoD)

As part of the UK's military 2011 intervention in Libya, the Trafalgar-class submarine, HMS *Triumph* fired her Tomahawk cruise missiles on three occasions. (DPL)

attached underneath), was on what is believed to have been a highly sensitive mission. A fire broke out on the Losharik on July 1, 2019, while it was taking underwater measurements of the sea floor in Russian territorial waters. The sub, which had only been launched in 2003, was designated as a special 'deep diving' surveillance sub. Fourteen members of the crew were killed by inhalation of smoke or toxic fumes.

The collapse of the Soviet Union in December 1991 generated a wave of change across the military. Russia became independent and together with Ukraine and Belarus, formed the Commonwealth of Independent States (CISS) before it later transitioned to become the Russian Federation.

New Nuclear Submarines
In July 2015, the then Commander in Chief of the Russian Navy, Admiral Viktor Chirkov, said: "The nuclear submarine fleet is the priority in the Navy shipbuilding program."

HMS *Turbulent* launched 30 Tomahawk cruise missiles prior to the Coalition land invasion of Iraq and when the sub returned to the UK, the crew flew the Jolly Roger. (EH/DPL)

A sailor aboard the Los Angeles-class fast-attack submarine USS *Jefferson City* loads a Mark 48 Advanced Capability (ADCAP) torpedo during an exercise. (US DoD)

The Northern Fleet inherited a lot of ageing vessels from the Soviet era, delivering little capability although they remained flying an ensign. In 2018, the Russian Ministry of Defence declared that the Northern Fleet was staging its biggest and most comprehensive series of naval exercises in recent years. Putin announced new submarines and at least five of Russia's most technologically advanced Yasen submarines for the Northern Fleet. A further four will serve with the Pacific fleet. Based on the design of the Akula- and Alfa-class, the Yasen-class will replace the Russian Navy's current Soviet-era nuclear attack submarines. A small number of the fleet's ageing Delta-class ballistic submarines are still being held in operational reserve to ensure Russia's Continuous at Sea Deterrent (CASD) can be maintained. The fleet's ballistic capability has ➲

officially been assigned to the new Borei-class, also known as the Dolgorukiy-class. The Borei boats are much smaller than the Typhoon boats they will replace. The huge 48,000-tonne Typhoon had a crew of 160 while the Borei is just 24,000 tonnes and operates with a crew of 107. But since the invasion of Ukraine in 2022, submarine development has almost ceased as the war soaks up financial resources. Elsewhere, North Korea is understood to have as many as 81 diesel-electric submarines, only one of them having the capability to launch ballistic missiles. It is estimated that 40 are Sang-O-class coastal submarines, 20 Romeo-class conventionally powered submarines, and 20 Yugo and Yono-class mini-submarines. The single diesel-electric ballistic missile submarine is known as the Gorae class.

Tension remains high between the North and the South (the Republic of Korea (ROK)), two countries that are officially still locked in conflict and have not agreed to any negotiation after the Korean War. ROK is seeking to expand its force, but as yet does not have nuclear boats. Since the 1990s, the backbone of the ROK's submarine fleet has been nine 1,200-tonne Chang Bogo-class diesel-electric attack submarines – a variant of the German Type 209 submarine. South Korea plans to upgrade all nine subs with air-independent propulsion (AIP). The ROK Navy is also in the process of acquiring nine German Type 214 — designated Son Won-II-class.

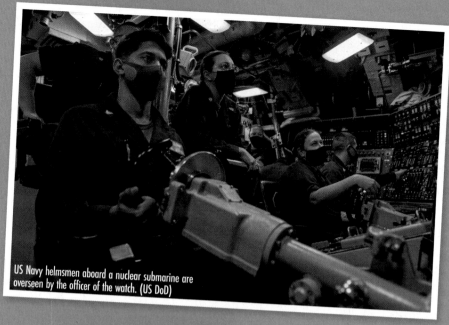

US Navy helmsmen aboard a nuclear submarine are overseen by the officer of the watch. (US DoD)

From South Africa to Bangladesh, Canada and across the globe, conventionally powered submarines remain in service with more than 50 countries and are seen as relevant to meet their nations' defence needs. The Russian Kilo-class has been a success story and is still in service with several platforms exported to India and Iran. Russia's neighbour and military ally, China, is building new conventional and nuclear submarines as it expands its force to strengthen Beijing's position in the Pacific.

Middle East Development
In the Middle East, the potential 'enemy below' is seen as Iran which continues to surge midget submarines into the Persian Gulf from the Republican Guard base in the Strait of Hormuz. In the early months of 2020, the US Navy warned that two submarines had deployed from Bandar Abbas, causing concern to commercial merchant ships. These small vessels, believed to be Ghadir-class, had been built in Iran and are designed to operate in the shallow waters of the Persian Gulf. They are operated by the Islamic Republic of Iran Navy and are in service with the Southern Fleet. The tactic used by the Ghadirs to restrict merchant ship traffic through the Strait of Hormuz is to sit on the surface, hidden among fishing fleets until a target is reported, then submerge to await their prey. In 2020, the then UK Defence secretary, Ben Wallace, ordered both HMS *Montrose*, a Type 23-class frigate, and HMS *Defender*, a Type 45-class destroyer, to resume 'close escort' patrols to protect UK merchant ships transiting through the Strait of Hormuz after tension with Iran. Former submarine captain, Commander Ryan Ramsay, who headed the nuclear hunter-killer boat HMS *Turbulent*, has stated that Iran's midget submarines are a threat with their Russian made Kilo-class boats being the most capable. He said: "The Iranian submarines can change the dynamic in the Strait of Hormuz

The huge size of a US nuclear submarine which is exposed to view during a refit. (US DoD)

A Seawolf-class SSN at Gibraltar. It was intended to be the replacement for the Los Angeles-class, but only three were built. (US DoD)

An artist's impression of an Ohio-class launching its missiles. These submarines will be replaced by the Columbia class which is due to enter service in 2031. (US DoD)

A Russian Borei-class filmed on the surface in the Barents Sea by a US surveillance aircraft. (US DoD)

put forward, but it is believed that the tubes are needed to launch the Israeli-developed Popeye cruise missiles. The US reportedly refused to sell Tomahawk cruise missiles, which would fit into the standard size torpedo tubes, so Israel developed their weapon based on the larger diameter Popeye air-launched missile. This has reportedly been test-fired in the Indian Ocean where it demonstrated a range of 1,500km. Even more controversial is that it is consistently reported that these missiles can be equipped with nuclear warheads (Israel is an undeclared but widely accepted nuclear power) giving the Dolphin-class a potential nuclear deterrence role.

Special Operations

The United States Navy has refurbished four nuclear ballistic missile (SSBN)

when they choose. The submarine force is a viable threat to shipping."

Israel maintains a small force of conventional boats for special missions. In the 1967 Arab Israeli war, the submarine INS *Tanin* deployed special forces to attack the Egyptian port at Alexandria. It then engaged an Egyptian frigate with torpedoes. The attack was thwarted and *Tanin* was subjected to depth charges. She escaped but was seriously damaged. Despite this, her captain took the boat back into Alexandria the next night with the aim of rescuing the commandos. Three Dolphin-class submarines were acquired by the Israel government, the INS *Dolphin*, INS *Leviathan* and INS *Tekumah* entering service in 1999. A degree of controversy surrounded the weapons' fit as the larger diameter 650mm torpedo tubes do not meet any standard Western weapon. Several suggestions have been

The Borei boats are much smaller than the Typhoons they will replace. (Russian DoD)

The UK operates four Vanguard (SSBN) submarines and is building a seven-strong fleet of Astute class (SSNs), plus it currently retains one Trafalgar-class hunter-killer boat in service. (UK MoD)

The US Navy has refurbished four nuclear ballistic missile (SSBN) Ohio-class submarines into guided missile (SSGN) submarines with additional accommodation for more than 60 troops. (US DoD)

Since the 1990s, the backbone of The Republic of Korea's submarine fleet has been a fleet of nine 1,200-ton Chang Bogo-class diesel-electric attack boats. (Korean DoD)

Ohio-class submarines into guided missile (SSGN) submarines and included additional accommodation to facilitate more than 60 troops. The US military sees special operations forces as critical to future littoral missions in which submarines need to take troops close to the coast without compromising their position, drop them off and loiter in the deep water until they need to recover the team. Future scenarios may well include the rescue of diplomats in countries under siege and as an advanced reconnaissance force ahead of a larger intervention.

New fast insertion craft which can be launched from a submarine, underwater dive vehicles and unmanned armed platforms to create, if needed, a diversion attack, are being procured by the Pentagon. Among the new developments being reviewed is a fast underwater craft that can travel in excess of 80nm, sitting just below the surface. It can dive, but long periods underwater reduce the endurance of the platform. Global flashpoints in the Gulf, the Pacific and off Africa are areas where US Navy SEAL teams could find themselves operating. To accommodate the

Iran continues to surge midget submarines into the Persian Gulf from the Republican Guard base in the Strait of Hormuz. (Iran MoD)

The US military sees special operations forces as critical to future littoral. (US DoD)

additional special operations forces, the team behind the refurbishing of the SSBNs to SSGNs knew they would have to fundamentally change the space within the submarine. They gutted one deck level of missile compartments to make room for special operations troops. The area now contains 66 berths and extra heads (toilets) facilities. Other additions include a large shower room where divers or others returning from a mission can use warm water to raise their body temperatures and a drying space in which to hang wet suits. The redesign also had to include space for the special operations forces' mission-specific equipment. Some of this can be stored in the main compartment where these troops sleep. Other equipment will be stored as payload in special operations forces canisters.

NATIONS WITH NUCLEAR CAPABILITY
United States: 72 – all nuclear powered – 54 SSNs, 14 SSBNs, 4 SSGNs
Russia: 73 – 13 SSBNs, 9 SSGNs, 51 diesel-electric
China: 69 – 12 nuclear powered, 4 SSBN, 6 SSNs; 47 conventionally powered (diesel-electric and AIP)
United Kingdom: 12 – all nuclear powered; 4 SSBN, 8 SSN
France: 8 – all nuclear powered; 4 SSBN, 4 SSN
India: 16 – 1 nuclear powered SSN (more planned); 15 conventionally powered (diesel-electric)

NATIONS BUILDING NUCLEAR CAPABILITY
Brazil: one being built. Nuclear powered (SSN).
Australia: 8 planned. Nuclear powered (SSN).

The canisters can be placed into torpedo tubes refitted to hold gear instead of weapons.

To prepare for submarine operations, Navy SEALs and other commandos with a maritime speciality have conducted realistic training exercises, such as escape trunk drills in pools or reservoirs and dockside training on moored submarines. Escape trunk drills are very important. Combat divers and submariners are placed in a 6ft spherical trunk that is flooded with water almost to the nose level. The trunk is placed at the bottom of the pool or reservoir. The person inside can breathe but is unable to do much more. Then the trunk's hatch is opened to flood the last few inches, immersing the person inside and forcing him or her to swim 30 or 40ft to the surface. This drill is used to simulate escaping from a crippled submarine. Locking out and locking in – respectively, exiting and re-entering a submerged submarine – are difficult operations, especially when conducted in the dead of night when the ocean is very dark. SEAL operators deploy in pairs and are tied together by a rope.

The US, Russia and China have embarked on building larger submarine forces, while the UK is building a replacement for the Vanguard SSBN. France is planning to replace its SSN force. India has plans to retire some of its diesel-electric force and build more nuclear vessels. ●

To prepare for submarine operations, Navy SEALs and other commandos with a maritime speciality conduct realistic training exercises. (US DoD)

MODERN SUBMARINES

S ubmarine warfare is about control of the deep oceans, protecting surface warships and finding the enemy before they locate you. Hunter-killer and attack submarines, classified as Sub Surface Nuclear (SSN), quietly 'stalk' their

adversary through the sonar orchestra of sub-surface noise – their trick is to 'go silent' and reduce all noise. Sonar operators aboard the boat sit monitoring screens and listening for the electronic signature of another submarine. If they locate a ping – the acoustic echo of another vessel – the commander may spend hours trying

to identify it. It is said that a sub commander will sometimes sit his submarine metres behind his foe's, shadowing every movement.

Technology is paramount to overcome the blindness of being in a submarine – it enables the crew to be aware of what is around them. Deep trenches, cables and shipwrecks can be plotted and

For the Sub Surface Nuclear (SSNs) attack boats, submarine warfare is all about control of the deep oceans, protecting surface warships and seeking out the enemy. (UK MoD)

allow the navigator to steer a safe passage. Such is the level of modern equipment that a crew can identify the class and often the name of another submarine from its acoustic signature. The noise from the propellor is, according to submariners, the DNA of a boat and unique to each vessel.

This is a dangerous environment and getting too close during a chase can result in collision. This is the 'vanguard' of the modern deep maritime battlespace, and the public know little about these top-secret operations. The Prime Minister is kept closely informed but only a handful of senior officers know where the ballistic boats deploy. In the 'black waters' of the Deep North and beyond, US and UK ballistic submarines mount their deterrent patrols in remote waters away from any Russian boats. The smaller SSNs quietly protect the much bigger vessels, known as bombers. They track and monitor Moscow's submarines and ensure that when they return to port in the US or the ➲

Submarine commanders quietly 'stalk' their adversary through the sonar orchestra of sub-surface noise. (US DoD)

Technology is paramount to overcome the blindness of being in a submarine deep under the ocean – it allows the crew to be aware of what is around them (DPL)

According to submariners, the noise generated by the propellor is unique to each vessel and is the DNA of a boat. (Russian MoD)

In the 'black waters' of the Deep North and beyond, US and UK ballistic submarines mount their deterrent patrols in remote waters where they aim to evade Russian boats. (DPL)

cancelled and after a long review, a new missile, Polaris, was procured and the deterrent passed to the Navy. By March 1982, the UK opted to buy the Trident II system as a generational replacement for Polaris, with the new missile planned to enter service in the 1990s.

The Trident D5 missile was assigned to the new ballistic submarine class, the Vanguard. At 16,000 tonnes and 150m long, this new vessel was the biggest submarine ever built in the UK. Four submarines were ordered with the requirement being that one boat remained at sea, departing from their base in Scotland. Meanwhile, the US has 18 Ohio-class subs in service, four of which have been converted to cruise missile carriers. The 18,700-tonne subs carry 24 Trident missiles. Submarines can travel any distance and respond to a range of threats that can include small autonomous platforms to major vessels.

The sub-surface world of warfare differs dramatically from surface operations. Below the water, there are no rules. Here when operational requirements demand, submarines can stalk inside the international waters of an adversary on missions never to be revealed and always denied.

UK, the Russians cannot get close. The hunter-killer and attack submarines are the workhorses of modern submarine operations.

The Nuclear Deterrent

Every day throughout the year, ballistic missile submarines from China, the US, Russia, France, and the UK drift along the seabed waiting for an adversary to launch an act of nuclear aggression. They are permanently on operations, remaining hidden and avoiding contact with surface ships. They rarely surface and are their country's most secret military assets.

For the US Navy and the Royal Navy (RN), the nuclear deterrent is based around the Trident II (or D5) missile. The system is currently deployed aboard the US Navy's Ohio ballistic-class submarines and RN's Vanguard-class boats. These weapons are carried when the boats deploy on patrol in a role known as the Continuous at Sea Deterrent (CASD) every day of the year. Trident is a three-stage, solid-fuelled submarine-launched ballistic missile. Since its introduction, the Trident D5 has undergone extensive improvement programs, including a more accurate global positioning system. The US Navy began developing the Trident D5 in March 1980. The first test launch took place in January 1987 and the first sea trial, which was unsuccessful, occurred in March 1989. The Trident D5 entered service in 1990, replacing the Polaris missile system which had entered service with the US Navy in 1961. Each submarine was armed with 16 missiles, powered by two solid-fuel stages. Polaris was also selected by the UK government and was in service with the RN from 1968 to 1996 after a decision was made to build a new generation of UK submarines and assign the nuclear deterrent to the Navy. The deterrent had been maintained by the RAF and was carried by Vulcan bombers but increases in radar and surface to air missiles made it apparent that aircraft bombers were increasingly vulnerable to attack and would be unlikely to penetrate Soviet airspace in the 1970s. At the same time, the concept of free-fall nuclear weapons was losing credibility, and the UK sought a ballistic missile. This was later

The smaller Sub Surface Nuclear (SSNs) quietly protect the much bigger vessels, known as bombers. (US DoD)

Crew members wear trainers which helps the noise down when they are moving around the sub. (US DoD)

Submarines can use their capability to monitor, eavesdrop and mount surveillance across the maritime, air and land environments, as well as deploy and extract special forces on sensitive missions. Often commanders can use their presence to fix the surface fleet of an adversary in port. Little is known about the exact deployments and operations of the silent service, but they are on operational duty from the minute they leave port. These unsung heroes rarely receive operational awards or campaign medals like other parts of the armed forces. The submarine service relies on its 'silence' and ability to stay hidden. From the Cold War to the actions in the Falklands, the true story of this force has leaked few secrets. While the shelves in bookshops are stacked high with books about special forces, few titles reveal the real life below the surface.

Sonar operators monitor a range of 'contacts' from commercial shipping to other submarines – logging distance, size, and speed of vessels as the submarine quietly manoeuvres below them. Successful operations rely on the skill of the commander and his number two – the executive officer – who must remain calm in the most serious of situations when the submarine is at depth and facing a crisis like a collision with the seabed, another submarine, a flood, or fire.

Submarine Command

Those who command ballistic submarines must be at the top of their game to be appointed to what is the most strategically important job ➲

China is developing a nuclear submarine force of ballistic and attack boats to expand its naval footprint in the Pacific. (PLAN)

a submarine's battery and during the mid-1980s Canada briefly considered the option of converting its Oberon-class submarines to nuclear power using a Slowpoke nuclear reactor, allowing it to continuously recharge the ship's batteries during submerged operations. Instead, it was decided to procure the Upholder-class submarines. Now, as the Victoria-class reach the end of their service, alternative options are being reviewed to power Canada's next generation of submarines. Among the systems being considered are off-the-shelf AIP submarines such as the French Barracuda Block 1A-class or the Japanese Soyru-class AIP design with lithium-ion battery (LIB) technology that extends the endurance of diesel submarines.

New diesel-electric attack AIP vessels are being procured by Italy, Norway and Germany, all NATO members, while Turkey has established its indigenous boat building programme. Algeria operates former Russia Kilo-class subs, while Azerbaijan lists its fleet as having midget submarines – although their serviceability is unclear. The definition of a midget submarine is any boat under 150 tonnes. They are typically operated by a small crew of three or four with the ability to ferry a six-man team of divers. Midget submarines have been widely used by global fleets.

Argentina is not known to operate midget submarines and list two vessels in its fleet – one a former US submarine and the second procured from Germany. Neither has been to sea for more than five years. They once had four boats – one was sunk by the British in the Falklands conflict (*Santa Fé*), the other, ARA *San Juan,* disappeared off the Argentine coast in November 2017, when it is presumed the boat suffered a major electrical failure.

Global Operators

Elsewhere, Bangladesh operates two former Chinese Ming-class submarines; Brazil operates German and French subs and is seeking to build its first nuclear vessel. Egypt operates four German 209-class boats and four former Chinese Romeo-classes. France operates a powerful force of four ballistic submarines and six nuclear attack boats. Greece operates 11 conventional subs, the newest being a German Type 214 – but budget restrictions have delayed refits to the fleet. India's submarine force includes the Arihant-class, the country's first nuclear powered ballistic boat. At one point, the Indian Navy leased two Akula boats from the Russians, but these have been returned. In addition, the fleet operates almost 18 conventionally powered submarines procured from Germany (Type 209-class), France (Scorpène class) and a Russian (Kilo class). Israel operates conventionally powered Dolphin-class boats, procured from Germany. Japan is expanding its submarine force and currently operates nine older Oyashio- class submarines, 12 Soryus and ➲

The Royal Navy Oberon-class diesel-electric submarine served in the Falklands and was retired and subsequently replaced with the Upholder class. (UK MoD)

Those who command ballistic submarines, such as the USS *Hamilton* pictured, must be at the top of their game to be appointed to what is the most strategically important role. (US DoD)

The Royal Navy diesel-electric Upholder-class submarine was sold to the Canadian fleet. (Canadian armed Forces)

The Argentine Type 209-class submarine ARA *San Juan* was lost in the South Atlantic. (Argentine Navy)

one Taigei-class. It has plans for two more Taigei-class submarines and is the only country in the world to use lithium batteries as a power source. The last two boats of the Soryu-class were fitted with lithium power as will be the Taigei.

Japan has conducted extensive research into the use of lithium-ion batteries on board submarines since the early 2000s and has found they require less maintenance and are capable

of longer endurance at high speeds while submerged, compared to lead-acid batteries.

Indonesia operates a small but growing submarine flotilla. In April 2019, two South Korean Daewoo-built vessels joined the fleet; they were named the Nagapasa class. A contract

for three more submarines was signed in 2019 with the completion of the final boat anticipated in 2026.

Iran lists 19 conventionally powered submarines in service and many midget vessels used for operations in the Gulf waters. Italy

Map showing the last position of the ARA *San Juan* in the South Atlantic.

Mar del Plata

Comodoro Rivadavia

Wreck

Ushuaia

Bangladesh operates two former Chinese Ming-class diesel-electric submarines. Observers claim they need significant maintenance and spend little time at sea. (US DoD)

An Egyptian Type 209 submarine under construction in Germany. (Egypt MoD)

operates eight attack submarines: Todaro and Sauro class. The Malaysian Navy operates two Scorpène-class subs, both procured from France and armed with Blackshark and Exocet SM-39 submarine-launched anti-ship missiles. The German Navy operates the Type 212-class which offer both diesel and an additional AIP system. The submarines can operate at high speed on diesel power or switch to the AIP system for

An Italian operator aboard a Todaro-class submarine during a NATO exercise. (Italian MoD)

silent slow cruising, staying submerged for up to three weeks with little exhaust heat. The Netherlands operates four Walrus conventionally powered submarines, which entered service in 1994. These small but highly effective boats often act as enemy forces for NATO wargames. The Dutch government plans to replace the Walrus in the next few years and has issued a tender requirement to three shipyards.

The North Korean government of Kim Jong Un has more than 80 vessels, including many midget submarines – including Yono and Sang-O class. It operates 20 Romeo-class vessels with at least one capable of deploying a small nuclear missile.

Pakistan established its submarine force in 1964. There are eight submarines in active service with the Pakistan Navy, including the Hashmat-class and Agosta-class, as well as three Italian midget vessels. The Hashmat-class submarines are equipped with an AIP system giving a capability of deeper dives and the ability to submerge for a longer period without detection. In 2014, the Pakistan Navy entered a joint venture project to procure Yuan-class submarines from China. The first vessels were due to enter service in 2023. In direct response to India's nuclear ballistic submarine force, Pakistan is now seeking to build its own vessels with the delivery of the first platform due in 2028.

China was the first Asian country and the fifth globally to successfully design, build and commission a nuclear-powered submarine. ⮑

The Dutch Walrus class diesel-electric submarine which is due to be replaced. (Netherlands MoD)

The People's Liberation Army Navy (PLAN) currently has two types of nuclear-powered attack submarines in service – the 093 and 091, with a third, the 095, in development. Submarine warfare is regarded as a vital part of PLAN's coastal defence doctrine. Large numbers of conventionally powered submarines have therefore been constructed and commissioned. China currently operates four different classes of conventional submarines. They are the Yuan-class or 039A, the Song-class or 039, the Kilo class, and the Ming or 035-class.

Submarine Forces

Taiwan maintains four submarines procured from Holland the United States. The Spanish Navy fields a small fleet of seven submarines based at the Cartagena naval base. They are three S-70 Galerna (Agosta class) and four AIP boats (S-80 class). In the Far East, Singapore acquired a Sjöormen-class submarine from the Swedish Navy in 1995 and another three in 1997 – they form the Challenger class. Before delivery, modifications were made to suit Singapore's demand and tropical waters. South Africa operates three German-built Type 209 which were delivered between 2004 and 2008 as a direct replacement for its Daphné-class submarines, The Type 209s from the Herine class. A new generation of submarines is being explored with Saab. The Turkish Navy has a 12 strong force of submarines. The Type 214-class vessels are regarded as a first for the Turkish Navy due to AIP by fuel cell technology.

In 2015, Gölcük Naval Shipyard began a ten-year programme to build six Type 214, locally known as Reis-class submarines with technology from ThyssenKrupp Marine Systems of Germany. In 2021, the Australian government, headed by PM Scott Morrison,

The Russian Navy operates several diesel-electric submarines, the newest and most popular being the Kilo class. (US DoD)

The Japanese Sōryū class diesel-electric submarine attack Hakuryū – the first of the new class to enter service. (Japan MoD)

Taiwan is building the new Hai Kun-class submarine which is believed to be based on the Dutch Zwaardvis class. (Taiwan Govt)

recently decided to join the nuclear submarine club – although the new Aussie boats will not carry nuclear weapons. A nuclear submarine force will be much faster and harder to detect in deeper water, than conventionally powered fleets, plus they can stay submerged for months, and launch missiles at greater distances. Australia will become just the seventh nation in the world to operate nuclear-powered submarines, after the US, UK, France, China, India, and Russia. The driving force behind the Australian decision is China's global rise supported by its increase in its military capability as Canberra faces Beijing's blunt pressure.

The Turkish Navy has a 12 strong force of Type 214-class vessels which operate air-independent propulsion and fuel cell technology. (NATO)

The Australian Navy currently operates the conventionally powered Collins class but is seeking nuclear powered boats under the AUKUS deal. (Australian MoD)

In 2018, the Australian government banned Chinese telecommunications company Huawei from its 5G networks. China's foreign ministry responded with a post on Twitter (now X) with a digitally enhanced image depicting an Australian soldier killing an Afghan child. In addition, the communist government retaliated with tariffs and trade restrictions against Australia after Prime Minister Morrison called for an independent inquiry about the origins of the Coronavirus. Morrison's government had been planning a diesel-electric fleet, but following a review, opted for nuclear power. The Australians also sought support from the United States and the Quadrilateral Security Dialogue – also known as the Quad – which is a strategic dialogue between the United States, India, Japan, and Australia initiated in 2007 by the then leaders of the four countries. This diplomatic and military arrangement was widely viewed as a response to increased Chinese economic and military power. China responded to the Quadrilateral dialogue by issuing formal diplomatic protests to its members. ●

THE RUSSIAN
BEAR

Russian naval commanders have for decades regarded their submarine fleet
as the 'jewel in the crown' of Moscow's combat power. (Russian MoD)

Cold War Legacy

RUSSIAN naval commanders have for decades regarded their submarine fleet as the 'jewel in the crown' of Moscow's combat power. They deploy submarines in the Baltic, the Black Sea and in the Pacific, as well as the mighty Northern Fleet. Based in the High North at Murmansk, this is the most capable force mounting patrols into the Atlantic, the Arctic Circle and beyond. The Northern Fleet is located at Severomorsk with six nearby bases at Polyarny, Olenya Bay, Gadzhiyevo, Vidyayevo – which includes Ura Bay and Ara Bay – as well as Bolshaya Lopatka, and Gremikha. The Barents Sea is their 'backyard' training area and gives them access to the Norwegian Sea, the Greenland Sea, the

Arctic Ocean, and the Kara Sea. North of the Barents Sea, Moscow has a base at the island Franz Josef Land and Novaya Zemlya. This is also home to thousands of Russian marines and special forces.

Since the collapse of the Soviet Union, the military has slowly been replacing its old Cold War submarines. In December 1991, Russia became independent and together with Ukraine and Belarus, formed the Commonwealth of Independent States (CISS) before it later transitioned to become the Russian Federation. By the early 1990s, President Boris Yeltsin's administration faced serious economic challenges, as well as a war in the breakaway republic of Chechnya. Russia's military influence across the globe was diluting fast

and Moscow's armed forces faced deep cuts, resulting in widespread cancellation of projects. The Northern Fleet, as did all the fleets, faced a review, which resulted in surface vessels being laid up or retired and the submarine force shrunk to just 79 vessels. This was still a major force compared to western submarine fleets, but the Russian force was not in good condition as refits and overhauls were delayed or cut short, and the lack of investment raised serious concern about the maintenance of the submarine fleet.

Cold War Legacy

In 1990, the Northern Fleet claimed to have 114 submarines, with 15 held in reserve. On paper the submarine fleet was impressive and ➲

included Typhoon- and Delta-class ballistic boats, Oscar class, Akula, Sierra, and Victor-class hunter-killers, as well as a force of Kilo-class conventional powered diesel subs.

At Sevastopol, home of the Black Sea fleet, a new revolutionary submarine was developed in the mid-1990s which commanders planned would serve with the Northern Fleet. But the sleek-looking Beluga, which included a closed-cycle air-independent propulsion (AIP) system, never made it to Murmansk. Instead, as financial cuts swept the fleet, the Beluga submarine was commissioned in 1998 and axed the same year. After the Cold War, the lack of planned maintenance periods was listed as a factor in several accidents. In the worst tragedy on August 12, 2000, the Russian nuclear-powered submarine *Kursk* was in an accident during naval exercises with the Northern Fleet in the Barents Sea. The entire 118-strong crew were lost aboard the Oscar II-class submarine which had only been built six years earlier in 1994. According to the Russian Navy, it had not been carrying nuclear warheads so there was never a danger of radiation leaks. A desperate Russian rescue operation took place in which other countries, including Britain, offered their assistance. The Russians were unable to establish radio communication with the stricken vessel, efforts by mini submarines sent to open the hatch repeatedly failed, costing valuable hours. The rescue operation was hampered by icy waters, stormy weather, and poor underwater visibility, as well as the Russians' slow arrival at the scene. It was claimed that some of the submarine's crew might have been rescued had the response been quicker, as the *Kursk* sank to the seafloor relatively close to the surface, at 350ft. The submarine's hull was recovered in 2021 and taken to a dry dock in Severomorsk, where the Northern Fleet were based. The bow was left on the seabed in the Barents Sea after engineers feared it would break up if lifted.

The mighty Northern Fleet is based in the High North at Murmansk. This is the most capable force mounting patrols into the Atlantic, the Arctic Circle and beyond. (Russian MoD)

Submariners serving with the Northern Fleet take part in a parade at Murmansk. (DPL)

President Vladimir Putin sees the High North as a future energy prize for Russia. (DPL)

The wreck was inspected by more than 20 teams under the direction of the Russian State Prosecutor General Vladimir Ustinov. On July 26, 2002, almost two years after the incident, General Ustinov announced his findings in a 133-volume report. It claimed that the hydrogen peroxide fuel in the dummy torpedo inside the fourth torpedo launcher set off the initial explosion that sank *Kursk*. Days later the Kremlin published a four-page summary supporting Ustinov's findings and claimed the accident was a direct result of 'stunning breaches of discipline, shoddy, obsolete and poorly maintained equipment'.

Ustinov's investigation determined that the failure of one of *Kursk*'s hydrogen peroxide-fuelled torpedoes triggered an explosion. It concluded that when the crew loaded a dummy torpedo – which allegedly had a faulty weld in its casing – that leaked high-test peroxide (HTP) inside the torpedo tube, initiating a catalytic explosion. The explosion blew off

Since the collapse of the Soviet Union, the military has slowly been replacing its old Cold War submarines. (Russian MoD)

Kilo-class submarines pictured at the Northern Fleet's Polyarny base in Murmansk. (Russian MoD)

both the inner and outer tube doors, ignited a fire, destroyed the bulkhead between the first and second compartments, damaged the control room in the second compartment, and incapacitated or killed the torpedo room and control-room crew. Two minutes and 15 seconds after the first explosion, another five to seven torpedo warheads exploded. They tore a large hole in the hull, collapsed bulkheads between the first three compartments and all the decks which destroyed compartment four, killing everyone still alive forward of the sixth compartment. The nuclear reactors shut down safely. The torpedo manufacturer challenged this hypothesis, insisting that its design would prevent the kind of event.

The report concluded that 23 sailors took refuge in the small ninth compartment and survived for more than six hours. When oxygen ran low, they attempted to replace a potassium superoxide chemical oxygen cartridge, but

Kilo-class conventional powered submarines form the backbone of the Black Sea fleet. (Russian MoD)

Dozens of old missile submarines were kept in service after the Cold War to boost the fleet's size – most have now been retired. (Russian MoD)

a $17.3 billion procurement upgrade. A year later in 2010, Vladimir Putin returned to power and ordered the Kremlin to press forward to boost the capability of the 'Russian Bear' with more state-of-the-art submarines. Putin wanted a force of 'special capabilities' submarines that no-one else had. These boats would be the instruments of state that Putin sought to influence his political policy and geopolitical aspirations.

War in Ukraine

In 2014 Putin's aggressive foreign policy began to emerge. His forces moved into the Crimea and the Donbass region of eastern Ukraine, sparking a conflict that attracted international outrage. That said, for many in the international community, annexation of Crimea was condemned but quickly forgotten.

Prior to the Russian seizure of the peninsula, the Kremlin was clearly preparing for conflict and announced a boost to the Black Sea fleet which would give Putin's forces the ability to control waters off Ukraine and if needed land forces by submarines and landing ships. As early as June 2010, Russian Navy Commander-in-Chief Admiral Vladimir Vysotsky announced plans for the modernisation of the Black Sea Fleet with 15 new warships and submarines. Then in 2021, more landing craft were sent into the Black Sea as Putin's naval commanders clearly prepared their forces for the invasion of Ukraine.

The wider Navy had been allocated a vast budget to fund Putin's pet project the 'special capabilities submarine' force, but the invasion of Ukraine quickly changed the direction of funding. The Russian operation in Crimea set the tone for Moscow's future plans. Kyiv feared the conflict in the Donbass would result in an invasion of mainland Ukraine. This was proven true when in February 2022, Russia mounted an illegal invasion. The Kremlin expected Kyiv to fall within days, but defenders fought back, hitting Putin's forces hard both on land and at sea. The cost of the fighting quickly became a financial drain on Moscow's defence

it fell into the oily seawater and exploded on contact. The resulting fire killed several crew members and triggered a flash fire which consumed the remaining oxygen, suffocating the remaining survivors. The disaster sparked intense public criticism of the government and the Russian Navy and left a stain on President Vladimir Putin's first term in office.

Several years later in 2008, 20 Russian submariners died when a Halon fire suppressant was accidently ignited aboard the *Nerpa*, an Akula-class nuclear submarine. The Halon gas was released inside two compartments of the submerged submarine during the vessel's sea trials in the Sea of Japan, asphyxiating the victims.

By 2003, the new President's administration revealed plans to fund a broad shipbuilding programme aimed at building a new 21st-century Northern Fleet. Funding was assigned for new warships and a series of new ballistic, hunter-killer, and conventional powered submarines. Then in 2009 the newly elected Russian President Dmitry Medvedev announced that the Russian Navy was to receive more than 30 ballistic missile submarines in

A Russian Project 659, Echo-class missile submarine – most were decommissioned by 1997. (Russian MoD)

Putin has been accused of using Russian submarine power as a weapon of his foreign policy. (Russian MoD)

In 2009 the newly elected Russian President Dmitry Medvedev announced that the Russian Navy was to receive more than 30 ballistic missile submarines in a new procurement. (Russian MoD)

budget and funding for the so-called 'special capabilities' submarines was reduced. While the war has mainly been a land domain operation, the Russian Navy's Black Sea fleet has been at the forefront of the naval action.

In 2022, the 4th Independent Submarine Brigade in the Black Sea Fleet included six conventionally powered Kilo-class boats: the *Alrosa, Novorossiysk, the Rostov-on Don, Starry Oskol, Novgorod* and the *Kolpino*. A seventh vessel, the *Krasnodar*, had been deployed to the Mediterranean. In March, just weeks after the war began, all six submarines went to sea in what was seen as an unprecedented event. The Kilo-class subs provided escorts for the surface fleet in the Black Sea which had been reinforced prior

to the war with amphibious vessels including landing ships and patrol ships, as well as the cruiser *Moskva*. While Ukraine has limited naval resources, Russia's submarines were the perfect platform from which to launch cruise missiles. Having fired, they could dive and exit their firing position. On May 15, 2022, four Kalibr missiles were launched from Kilo-class submarines in the Black Sea, with the Russians claiming the missiles hit Ukrainian military facilities near Lviv. The Kalibr is a land-attack cruise missile with an estimated

range of around 1,600 miles and has become a mainstay in the Russian Navy's ground-strike capabilities.

Two days later, on May 17, 2022, the Ministry of Defence of the Russian Federation reported that submarine-fired Kalibr missiles struck railway facilities at Starychi station near Lviv the night before. The attack was aimed at NATO weapons deliveries to Ukraine. Lviv Oblast Governor Maxim Kozitsky confirmed the damage to railway infrastructure while the commander of the Ukrainian Air Defence ➲

Russia's naval sources claim that at least one Typhoon ballistic submarine remains in service. (Russian MoD)

claimed the shooting down of three missiles in the area.

On September 13, 2023, Ukraine alleged that it had used a Storm Shadow long-range cruise missile in a strike against the Sevastopol port, which seriously damaged the submarine *Rostov-on-Don*. Almost a year later, on August 3, 2024, Ukraine used a long-range cruise missile to hit and subsequently sink the same sub which had returned to Sevastopol for maintenance.

Since 2022 Russia submarine activity in the Northern North Sea has reduced, but the boats that deploy continue to try and harass UK naval assets. In September 2024, the Royal Navy deployed the Type 23 frigates HMS *Iron Duke* and HMS *Tyne* to track a Kilo submarine (which was on the surface), and three Russian warships through UK waters. The shadowing of the Russian vessels was an Alliance operation with Canadian and Belgian warships joining in the mission to monitor the Kilo class sub. The move came amid growing tension between Moscow and the West over the war in Ukraine. At the time of the incident, the Kremlin mouthpiece and former Russian President, Dmitry Medvedev, threatened to 'sink' Britain. On social media he posted: "Our hypersonic missiles will help if necessary." And Putin has himself warned that Britain and other Western backers of Ukraine face the harshest of consequences if they permit Ukraine to unleash NATO-supplied long-range missiles at military targets deep inside Russia.

New Developments

Plans for the Borei SSBN-class boats started shortly after the fall of the Soviet Union with the first hull being laid in 1996. But progress was plagued by financial cutbacks and a series of challenges in the development of the Bulava missile. The first Borei was commissioned in 2007, but it was not until 2011 that the first of the class, *Yury Dolgoruky* (K-535), fired a test missile and joined the fleet in the same year. Finally, in 2014, 18 years after being built, the first of class was deployed on operations. The Borei has a crew of 130, operates a single shaft propelled system and has a speed of 25kts. Critical to their operational effectiveness is the submarine's underwater 'sonar footprint' – the noise it generates – and Moscow claims the Borei is five times quieter than any other modern submarine.

The new generation of attack submarines, the Sub-Surface Nuclear (SSN) Yasen class, will deliver new capability to the fleet. Construction on the first one started in 1993 with the first of class, the *Severodvinsk* (K-560), entering service in December 2013. Moscow claims the 8,600-tonne subs are undetectable, although US Naval intelligence claimed they quickly located and tracked the first boat. Two more of the

The Northern Fleet is the most prestigious of Russia's operational forces, with more than 45,000 personnel based in the Murmansk region. (Russia MoD)

class, the *Kazan* (K-561) and the *Novosibirsk* (K-573), have joined the fleet. These submarines carry a limited crew of just 64 and are armed with the Kalibr long-range cruise missiles. In total, the Kremlin issued plans to build nine, five of which are expected to join the Northern Fleet. US Navy commanders have said that the Yasen is a potent submarine, and Russian officials indicated that in the summer of 2018 the Severodvinsk operated in the Atlantic for several weeks. The Russian Navy also has four Khabarovsk-class strategic submarines being built (known as Project 09851), which will carry a new, unlimited range Poseidon nuclear missile system that's capable of hitting the United States. These 10,000 tonne subs will be built to the same specification as the Borei class but will be much smaller.

Special Operations Missions

Moscow pioneered new submarine operations and deployed a 'special missions' vessel called the Belgorod in 2022. The submarine, a modified version of Russia's Oscar II-class guided-missile submarine, was extended to become the world's longest submarine in readiness to accommodate the world's largest torpedo, the *Poseidon*. It is a nuclear powered,

A Russian Akula class with its distinctive tail section. There are four classes of Akula (Project 971) launched between 1984 and 2009. (Russian MoD).

A Kilo submarine of the Black Sea Fleet pictured in Sevastopol. One of these vessels was destroyed by a Ukrainian missile in 2024. (Russian MoD)

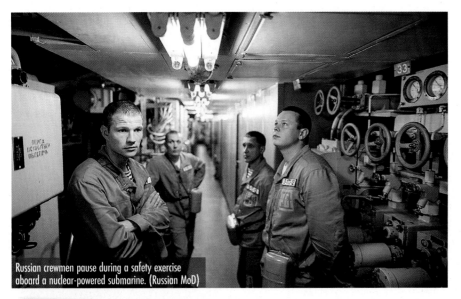

Russian crewmen pause during a safety exercise aboard a nuclear-powered submarine. (Russian MoD)

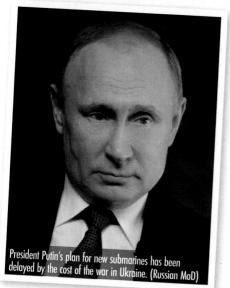

President Putin's plan for new submarines has been delayed by the cost of the war in Ukraine. (Russian MoD)

flood lights, remotely operated arms to manage equipment, and retractable ski feet for sitting on the seabed. Although described as a scientific research submarine, she is also assigned to the GUGI. In 2019, a special mission platform deployed with submarine attached. Some reports suggested the 'mother sub' was the Belgorod, but others indicated it was the *Podmoskovye*. Within days of the start of the deployment, a fire broke out on the Losharik on July 1, 2019. At the time the submarine was taking underwater measurements of the sea floor in Russian territorial waters. In total 14 members of the crew were killed by inhalation of smoke or toxic fumes. According to official reports, *Losharik* is now in Severomorsk, the headquarters of the Russian Fleet, awaiting repair. To date, it is unclear what has happened to the Belgorod or the *Podmoskovye*. In April 2021, the Russian Defence Ministry allegedly sent the Belgorod into service with Moscow's Pacific Fleet.

New Threats

The arrival of new ballistic and hunter-killer submarines signalled a surge in activity in operational activity as the newly refurbished Murmansk-based force flexed its military muscle. In 2017, Admiral Vladimir Korolyov, ➲

carry the Poseidon nuclear torpedo. Russian Navy briefings indicate her role was primarily to carry a smaller submarine at the base of her hull. This was the Losharik – specially developed to dive into the extreme depths of the Arctic. This sub, built with a titanium hull, was designed to operate on the ocean floor with front-mounted

nuclear-armed autonomous torpedo that can travel at speeds of up to 185km/h. It has a range of 10,000km and can operate at depths of up to 1,000m. The Poseidon is armed with a two-megaton nuclear warhead and can be used to target coastal cities and naval bases, as well as carrying equipment for intelligence gathering. The Belgorod is 60ft long longer even than the US Navy's Ohio-class ballistic and guided missile submarines. Operated by the Main Directorate of Deep-Sea Research (known as the GUGI), the Belgorod also has the ability to attach smaller 'special operations' midget subs under her hull, including the revolutionary Losharik, a deep diving vessel which was designed operate in the 'ultra deep' waters of the High North. The Belgorod was also reported to have the ability to deploy a swarm of mini-robot subs that could move along the seabed and carry out deep reconnaissance.

A second submarine, the *Podmoskovye*, a former Delta IV class SSBN, was also modified to support Putin's 'special mission project'. The main focus of these huge submarines was to deliver and escort smaller deep-dive manned vessels to investigate energy resources in the High North as well as the future control of the increasingly important sea trade route through the Arctic due to the melting ice. The focus for the *Podmoskovye* was similar to the Belgorod – although it is unclear if the *Podmoskovye* can

Sailors who signed up to become submariners with the Northern Fleet have found themselves transferred to missile regiments and sent to Ukraine. (Russian MoD)

The Delta-class submarines dominated in the Northern Fleet with more than 20 in service before they were retired in 2004. (Russian MoD)

The *Alexander Nevsky*, one of Moscow's most advanced Borei-class nuclear powered submarines, designation Project 955. (Russian MoD)

Intelligence) vessel. In October 2019, it was revealed that Norway's military intelligence agency, the Norwegian Intelligence Service (NIS), had monitored the largest single Russian submarine exercise since the end of the Cold War, involving at least ten submarines. Then in early 2020, it was claimed that the US Navy had spent weeks trawling the North Atlantic in the hunt for a Russian submarine that was known to have deployed into the waters off the east coast of the United States

NATO's Concern

NATO's biggest concern in the 21st century is directed at undersea cables and energy pipelines. Since the invasion of Ukraine, Moscow has quietly escalated a hybrid war against the West. In September 2022 four explosions ruptured the Nord Stream gas pipeline which sits on the seabed at a depth of 360ft and runs from Russia through the Baltic Sea to Germany. The Russian salvage ship SS-750, with its mini-submarine, was observed by the Royal Danish Navy at the site of the sabotage four days before the explosions. On November 18, 2022, the Swedish Security Service concluded that the incident was an act of "gross sabotage", stating that traces of

who had taken command of the Russian Navy in 2016, claimed his submarine crews had spent more than 3,000 days on patrol in that year. This renewed capability included a fleet of overhauled and repaired older vessels such as the four Oscar IIs in service with the Northern fleet and at least two Delta IVs. The focus of this group may well have been an area known as the 'Greenland Gap' – the waters between the UK, Iceland, and Greenland, which are strategically important. In a direct response to the surge in Russian submarine activity, the US Navy re-established its Second Fleet in 2018. Its area of responsibility being the North Atlantic Ocean, the region where the Russian Northern Fleet had been operating with increasing frequency at a level not seen since the Cold War. At the time, Admiral John Richardson, the then chief of naval operations, said: "The best way to avoid a fight is to develop the most powerful and deadly, competitive Navy possible."

The 21st century has also seen a spike in submarine and spy ships of the Northern Fleet across the Atlantic as the Kremlin seeks to expand its surveillance footprint. In December

2019, a Russian spy ship was tracked by US maritime authorities as it loitered off the southeastern coast of the United States. The vessel, the *Viktor Leonov*, was known to be a Russian Vishnya-class surveillance ship, also known as an AGI (Auxiliary Gathering

The Victor-class submarine first entered service in 1967, and the upgraded Victor III remains in service, although its operational readiness is unclear. (Russian MoD)

The Northern Fleet has invested in new ice ships to support Moscow's ambitious plans to establish a foothold in the High North and harness oil and gas resources. (Russian MoD)

A Russian Kilo-class conventionally powered submarine pictured in the North Atlantic by a NATO surveillance aircraft. (NATO)

explosives were found on the pipes. The Danish Defence Command then confirmed that six Russian navy ships, including the SS-750, were operating in the area four days before the explosion.

Hundreds of sub-sea cables run across the world's seas and oceans, with cables in the Atlantic Ocean and the North Sea seen as being exposed to Russian sabotage. In addition, gas pipelines that supply Europe are largely unguarded and their exact positions are in the public domain. Since the invasion of Ukraine, reports of suspicious Russian activity close to undersea cables have increased. This threat to underwater infrastructure is viewed as one of the many tools in a far broader Kremlin toolbox of hybrid warfare methods against the West. In spring 2024, the UK, Netherlands, Belgium, Germany, Norway, and Denmark signed an agreement to protect critical underwater infrastructure in the North Sea

Putin's powerful modern nuclear and diesel-electric powered submarines at the annual Navy Day celebrations. (Russian MoD)

Putin and his military commanders at a naval parade. (Russian MoD)

from potential Russian sabotage. The move came amid recognition that the North Sea now serves as a critical hub connecting European countries through power cables, gas pipelines, and telecommunications links. In September 2024, CIA and MI6 chiefs accused Russia of engaging in a 'reckless campaign of sabotage' across Europe. Alleged recent Russian attacks on communications systems have included disruption to the Global Positioning System (GPS) that affected thousands of civilian passenger flights in the Baltic Sea, Black Sea, and eastern Mediterranean regions. Alarm over the security of the world's vital undersea communications arteries comes as concern mounts over a possible further escalation in Russia's hybrid war. The Kremlin is believed to be considering a variety of options as it looks to retaliate for Western military support provided to Ukraine. While direct military action is viewed as unlikely, attacks on critical infrastructure could cause chaos and impose significant costs. ●

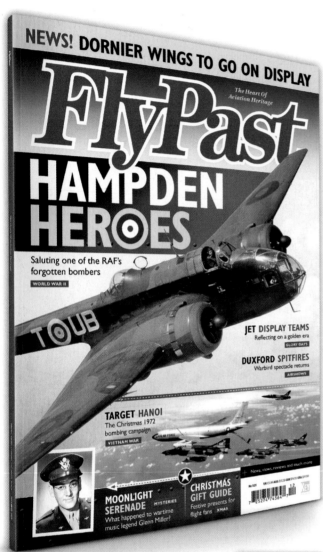

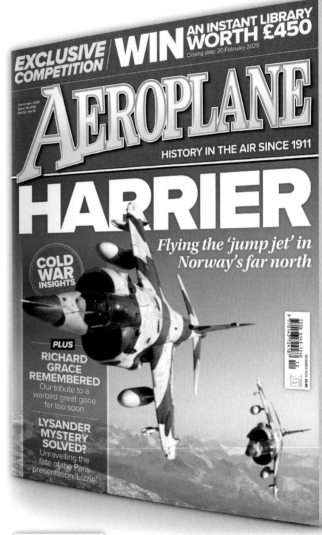

SUBSCRIBE TODAY!

collections/subscriptions

Free 2nd class P&P on BFPO orders. Overseas charges apply.

ASIA AND THE RISE OF THE DRAGON

China is modernising its submarine force with Type 39A Yuan-class submarines, pictured, and new nuclear boats. (PLAN)

The waters of the Asian Pacific are seen as a potential flashpoint area for future submarine conflict. While these international waters are regularly visited by submarines from the United States, Britain, and Australia as well as India, they are dominated by China's fleet. Here Beijing constantly claims sovereignty of the South China Sea and seeks to illegally enforce control of international shipping lanes used by global merchant ships. At the same time, China constantly flexes its military might to inform the world that it plans to reunify Taiwan – stating that if needed, it will use force.

Meanwhile, North Korea continues to threaten regional stability with its isolationist policy and frequent missile tests, while Vietnam, Indonesia and the Philippines continue to protest to the President Xi Jinping administration about the ongoing damage to their economies as their powerful neighbour ignores international agreements and prevents regional fishermen from accessing fishing grounds.

The submarine is well suited to the waters of the Pacific – the largest

Western governments fear an economic and military alliance between Presidents Xi Jinping and Vladimir Putin. (PLAN)

and deepest ocean on earth, covering more than 60 million square miles and averaging a depth of 13,000ft. This ocean is strategically important to the US, China, Australia, and the Pacific Island countries that sit along the coast. Washington has long maintained influence and a military presence in the Pacific, while in the past decade, China has focused on broadening its footprint in the Pacific Rim, through increased financial aid – often in return for naval access – as well as arrogant diplomacy and enforced attempts to take ownership of remote and artificial islands.

The Pacific Rim

Growth in maritime capability is central to Beijing's bold economic ambitions and the 'Rise of the Dragon' to control trade in the Pacific Rim – the area of countries that lie along the Pacific Ocean. Access to global oceans is critical to the West's economy, but China sees control of these waterways – such as the South China Sea – as being critical to its future growth and power. Beijing's strategy is increasingly seen as adopting an aggressive and intimidating posture towards its neighbours. In just over four decades the People's Liberation Army Navy (PLAN) has developed a strong blue-water fleet and today its focus is on submarine capability. To protect its waters, PLAN operates three fleets: the North Sea Fleet is based in the Yellow Sea with its headquarters in Qingdao Shandong Province; the East Sea Fleet covers the East China Fleet and operates from Ningbo in Zhejiang Province; the South Sea Fleet is deployed from a base at Zhanjiang in Guangdong Province.

Every two years the countries of the region stage Exercise Pacific Rim. The aim is to prepare nations for a variety of scenarios and form a coalition to maintain stability in ⮑

While the United States was the first to develop a nuclear submarine, it took China almost two decades to build their first nuclear boat and upgrade their conventional force. (PLAN)

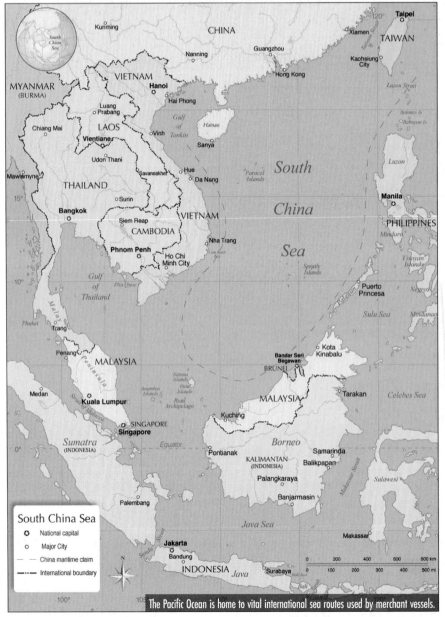

The Pacific Ocean is home to vital international sea routes used by merchant vessels.

the Pacific. It represents the world's biggest naval manoeuvres, with the obvious aim of deterring Chinese expansion. In 2014 China was invited to participate in the biennial Rim of the Pacific naval exercise. It sent four ships as well as an uninvited spy ship and offered little co-operation. In 2024, 29 partner nations joined the military exercise – the biggest ever – but China did not receive an invite as a result of what Washington described as its "reluctance to adhere to international rules or norms and standards". A US Navy spokesman said: "The US invited China in 2014 with hopes that it might stop its militarisation of the South China Sea and realise that engaging in great power competition was futile."

China maintains its information war in the region, forcing Western fleets to visit the region to exercise their right of passage in international. Such events can be

Chinese submariners are paid slightly more than those serving in the surface fleet and enjoy limited privileges. (PLAN)

subsonic missile which has an estimated range of 330 miles.

For the past 20 years, the US Navy has dominated in the Pacific, but that dynamic is changing as Beijing is working hard to change the 'military balance'. President Xi Jinping shows no sign of reducing his country's investment in the PLAN's naval power. During the same period, the communist regime has procured a wide range of vessels, including 40 new submarines, adding to the fleet's powerful force.

New Submarines in the Region

The Chinese navy has reconfigured its new generation Jin class, Type 094, submarines, capable of firing ballistic missiles that can reach the US mainland. Their design, according to experts, will make them subs stealthier and quieter. This race for global military superiority has seen the PLAN's submarine service given priority as the country seeks ⟳

Routine drills are carried out to prepare the crew for any incident from fire to toxic fumes. (PLAN)

highly controversial but are carried out to ensure that merchant vessels can continue use these seas lanes to transit commercial goods to and from Europe. In 2021 the UK deployed an unnamed attack submarine to protect the carrier HMS *Queen Elizabeth* when she deployed to the Pacific to take part in international wargames. The carrier entered the disputed South China Sea to conduct Freedom of Navigation exercises alongside the US Navy in international waters. It is understood that during the deployment, submarines from the US, France and Holland joined the UK boat in protecting the carrier. At the same time, it was revealed that China was testing its new so-called carrier-killer DF-21D anti-ship missiles. The tests were carried out on land and Beijing is also said to have been developing a new submarine-based system to replace the YJ-18

Western forces regularly transit the South China Sea to enforce their right to travel through international waters. (US DoD)

The Royal Navy's aircraft carrier HMS *Queen Elizabeth* has deployed to the Pacific and her sister vessel *Prince of Wales* will travel to the region in 2025. (UK MoD)

A US Navy task force exercises its right to passage through the South China Sea. (US DoD)

super power status. Little is known about the PLAN's submarine tactics, but much of their training and operating procedures have been adopted from the Russian Navy. Between 1960 and 1985, China is understood to have built more than 80 Romeo-class (Type 33) attack submarines, as well as several Ming class (Type 35). The first ballistic missile submarine (SSBN) to be designed and built in Asia was a Chinese Xia-class (Type 092). The submarine was commissioned in 1982 and entered into service in 1987. But the Xia class was slow and noisy and was quickly replaced by the Jin class (Type 094). The Shang-class submarines (Type 093) closely resemble the former Soviet Victor III submarine. They entered service in 2006 and six remain in service. In the same year, the Yuan-class joined the fleet. It was the PLAN's first class of diesel-electric submarine to be equipped with an indigenously developed air-independent propulsion system (AIP).

China has agreed to purchase four Lada-class (Project 677E) diesel-electric attack submarines from Russia. (The Russian export version is known as Amur-1650.) The first Lada-class submarine was reportedly delivered in 2014. It is believed to be one of Russia's most modern conventional subs – an upgrade of the Kilo class.

The PLAN commissioned three upgraded Shang-class (Type 093B) nuclear-powered attack submarines in 2015. The advanced Shang-class offers improvements in speed and noise, as well as a new vertical launch system. The vessels carry

US Navy aircraft carriers have been challenged by Chinese warships and warned that submarines are tracking them. (US DoD)

A Royal Navy Astute-class submarine has transited through the Pacific in its role escorting the carrier. (UK MoD)

the advanced YJ-18 anti-ship ballistic missiles. Washington estimates that by the mid-2020s China will likely construct the Type 093B guided-missile nuclear attack submarine (SSGN), a new variant of the Shang-class that would improve anti-surface warfare capability. China is also understood to be building more SSBNs.

In September 2024, China's newest nuclear-powered attack submarine was reported to have sunk in its dock earlier this year while under construction. The boat was understood to be one of Beijing's new Zhou-class in a major setback for the Chinese military. US analysts suggested it was probably a Type 041 Zhou class though it could also be a modified Type 039, a conventionally powered Air Independent Propulsion (AIP) boat. Satellite images taken in June show what appear to be floating salvage cranes at the berth in Wuhan where, a month previously, the vessel had been seen. Beijing has not confirmed the reports and declined to confirm if it was a nuclear or diesel-electric sub. The sinking comes at a time when Beijing has been increasingly assertive in laying claim to virtually the whole of the South China Sea – an area which is crucial to international trade. It has long-standing maritime disputes

with other nations in the region, including Brunei, Malaysia, the Philippines, Taiwan, and Vietnam.

Across the region, India, Pakistan, and North Korea maintain operational submarines and according to an International Institute for Strategic Studies investigation in 2024, India has 16 operational submarines – including five French Scorpène-class boats (renamed Kalvari class), four German Type 209s (named as the Shishumar class) and seven Russian Kilos, named as the Sindhugosh class, as well as two nuclear ballistic submarines. In addition, the fleet has accepted the ballistic boats INS *Arihant* and INS *Arighaat* – although critics have suggested that a lack of funding is restricting the operational capability of the Indian fleet.

Pakistan has ordered eight Hangor-class diesel-electric Air Independent Propulsion ➲

The PLAN's reconfigured new generation Jin class Type 094 submarines are capable of firing ballistic missiles that can reach the US mainland. (PLAN)

powered submarines from China to bolster its force – the first is due to be delivered in 2025. It currently operates two Agosta 70-class boats purchased from France and three Agosta-90B boats. In 2003, the then Chief of the Naval Staff, Admiral Shahid Karimullah, stated that Pakistan had no intentions to arm its submarines with nuclear warheads unless it felt threatened by India. Then, in January 2017, Pakistan successfully test-fired its first nuclear-capable submarine-launched cruise missile, the Babur-3. Pakistan tested the Babur-3 missile again in April 2018, but as yet shows no intent to deploy them at sea. Most of Pakistan's submarines are based at the Karachi Naval dockyard, although there are plans to base some vessels at Jinnah Naval Base in Ormara, west of Karachi.

South Korea operates 18 non-nuclear submarines while its neighbour North Korea

This race for global military superiority has seen the PLAN's submarine service given priority as the country seeks super power status. (PLAN)

There are currently three Type 091 Han-class submarines held in the reserve fleet. (PLAN)

operates one of the world's largest fleets with an estimated 71 vessels in service. Many are old and it is understood that only one can fire nuclear weapons, with the most recent test-firing taking place in October 2021. Japan operates six submarine squadrons of diesel-electric boats with an estimated 40 vessels in service. Vietnam operates six Kilo-class submarines, while the Republic of China (ROC) Taiwan Navy currently has four diesel-electric submarines and is planning to build eight more. Malaysia operates two diesel-electric Scorpène-class subs. Meanwhile, the Philippines has recently announced its plans to procure its first submarine.

Naval Capability

Concerns about future stability in the region have resulted in Japan and other countries

China holds regular parades for submariners, similar to those held in Moscow, which are designed to generate public support for the armed forces and the country. (PLAN)

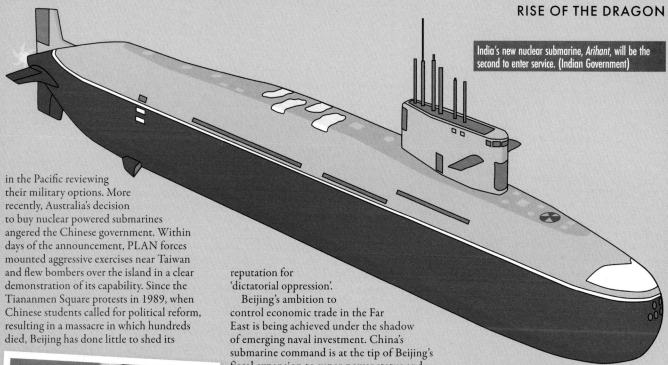

India's new nuclear submarine, *Arihant*, will be the second to enter service. (Indian Government)

in the Pacific reviewing their military options. More recently, Australia's decision to buy nuclear powered submarines angered the Chinese government. Within days of the announcement, PLAN forces mounted aggressive exercises near Taiwan and flew bombers over the island in a clear demonstration of its capability. Since the Tiananmen Square protests in 1989, when Chinese students called for political reform, resulting in a massacre in which hundreds died, Beijing has done little to shed its

President Xi Jinping has focused his defence spending on new submarines and missile systems that can reach the United States. (PLAN)

reputation for 'dictatorial oppression'.

Beijing's ambition to control economic trade in the Far East is being achieved under the shadow of emerging naval investment. China's submarine command is at the tip of Beijing's fiscal expansion to super-power status and global prominence – generated by growing political and trade pressures as well as the COVID-19 pandemic which have fuelled an arms race to build forces to dominate the region. Beijing is developing its collaboration with Moscow and their forces are pressing hard to undermine western political influence in Asia and the Far East.

This race for global military superiority has seen the PLAN's submarine service take centre stage as the country aims to become a world power. President Xi Jinping has set an agenda for his people to see their country as a 'Wolf Nation'. He came to office in 2013 and quickly made it clear that he planned to expand China's economy by securing trade across the Pacific and use military force to safeguard his plans – particularly in areas such as the South China Sea. His economic drive has refocussed on the reunification of Taiwan and the demise of American influence in the Far East.

South China Sea

Beijing constantly promotes its claim to sovereignty of the international waterway which is also claimed by Vietnam, Taiwan, Malaysia, Brunei, the Philippines, and Japan. These coastal countries rely on the huge fishing fields to support their economies, which China increasingly polices with armed coastguard ships. Tension in the region was further spiked after China developed two island chains, spending millions to recover land from the sea. These artificial islands, called the Paracel and Spratly, are now home to Chinese military forces armed with missiles and radar units. The Paracel islands sit to the north of the South China Sea and the Spratly in the south, giving the Chinese military two important strategic bases in the waterway. In the past five years, PLAN warships have regularly challenged foreign warships that transit these international shipping lanes, claiming the area is part of China's ➲

Controlling trade across the Pacific and to the West is at the heart of Beijing's plan to build its economy and rise as a world power. (PLAN)

The AUKUS project will see Canberra supplied with US Virginia-class submarines and British technology. (US DoD)

New boats are expected to be built in Australia with Royal Navy and US personnel providing training. (US DoD)

sovereign territory. Beijing is attempting to spread its political agenda, aiming to expand its capability with plans for new overseas bases to provide naval support facilities for Chinese naval power beyond the Pacific. This huge investment comes as the communist party seeks to project control across the Pacific and beyond to control maritime trade and secure its future economy. Beijing has overtly embarked on a programme of 'peaceful' expansion' while mounting an information campaign aimed at intimidating its neighbours and Western nations. This policy has undermined stability in the region and fuelled an explosive tension across the Far East with the US deploying military assets which are at constant readiness in the area.

The Threat to Taiwan

The Chinese administration regards Taiwan as a breakaway province and seeks to reunify the island to mainland China – warning that it does not rule out an invasion. It holds frequent naval exercises to remind the island's administration of its power and has warned allies of Taiwan that they should stand back. Taiwan's President Lai Ching-te has said he wants his country to remain independent, strong, confident, and ready to deal with any predators. The country, which calls itself the Republic of China, can field a navy of 69 active warships and four conventionally powered submarines. These include two Hai Shih- and two Chien-class boats, while further indigenous built submarines will boost the total to 12. The first of these new vessels will enter service in late 2024 and this modest naval force will face a Beijing force of more than 300 warships and over 80 submarines.

The tension and potential threat of conflict between China and Taiwan is very real. Beijing views its national security as being intrinsically linked to the island and the Chinese Communist Party has stated for more than seven decades that it will secure the unification of the island by negotiation or military action. The driving factors for China's increasing impatience include the apparent growing lack of support among the Taiwanese people, particularly the young, for a union with China. Xi Jinping's ambition is to secure his legacy and become the Chinese leader who reunited the island, while Washington continues to offer its military and political assistance for the island.

The trilateral partnership of Australia, the UK, and US, known as AUKUS, has been developed to equip the Australian Navy with new nuclear-powered submarines – although these vessels will not carry nuclear weapons. The agreement has not been welcomed in Beijing – especially as Washington has been constantly calling for China to pull back its military expansion. However, it is highly unlikely that the US will commit its armed forces to offensive action in what will potentially result in a state-on-state war. Instead, it is much more likely to provide Taiwan with more military equipment as

An artist's impression of the new Virginia class which will serve with the Australian Navy. (US DoD)

well as intelligence and surveillance assets to allow them to fight back. In addition, any conflict would also see Beijing being hit with economic sanctions – tariffs on Chinese goods into the US which would have a major impact on China's economic ambitions. Prior to the

pandemic, the United States' imports totalled more than $400bn while exports amounted to less than $150bn – a significant figure for China. In 2023 the total value of Chinese exports to the US had soared to £501bn, while imports from America was listed at $147bn. ➲

In the South China Sea, the Chinese have also built on the reefs and based naval forces on these artificial land masses. (US DoD)

In mainland China numerous government hawks see Beijing's power growing. Victor Gao, vice president of the Centre for China and Globalisation, warned that China will unify Taiwan and has expressed his concern at the growing strategic alliance between the US, Australia, and the UK. He said: "The unification of China is a must; it must happen. If peaceful means cannot be achieved, then any means is possible. It is not an invasion it is a unification of the motherland. The West should wake up and realise that no country can stand in our way. Look how America ran away from Afghanistan, they will not send their soldiers to die in the defence of Taiwan." Taiwan's former President, Tsai Ing-wen, feared that intervention by China will have a serious impact on the region. She said: "If Taiwan were to fall, the consequences would be catastrophic for regional peace."

China's Growing Force

While Washington openly supports the government in Taipei, the US has sought to build diplomatic relations with Beijing, which were strained during the Trump period of office. According to intelligence analysts in Washington, since 2002, China has built ten new nuclear submarines (six Shang class and four Jin). It was alleged in documents posted on the internet that China is developing a new hi-tech nuclear power attack submarine, however

The US Navy carrier Carl Vinson transiting through the South China Sea. (US DoD)

Beijing has declined to make any comment. The force consists of six ballistic (SSBN) boats of the Jin-class, known as Type 094). These vessels are 135m long and carry 12 JL-2 SLBMs. Six Shang-class, known as Type 093, nuclear powered attacks subs (SSNs) can allegedly reach speeds up to 30kts and are armed with cruise missiles. Its 48-strong diesel electric subs (SSKs) include

Kilo, Song and Ming-class vessels and there are a further 40 air independent subs (AIP) of the Yuan class (Type 039 and Type 041).

China's diesel-electric submarines have considerable capability. In October 2006, a Song-class diesel-electric submarine surfaced within five miles of the aircraft carrier USS *Kitty Hawk* during a US naval exercise off Okinawa in the Pacific. The incident raised questions in the Pentagon about the Chinese vessel's ability to evade the anti-submarine systems of US ships escorting the carrier. Nine years later, in 2015, a Chinese Kilo-class shadowed the aircraft carrier USS *Ronald Reagan* off the coast of Japan.

Chinese Submarines in summary

Jin-class (Type 094) ballistic missile submarines (SSBNs) are 135m long with a 12.5m-wide beam and can travel over 20kts when submerged. Their weapons systems can carry 12 JL-2 SLBM intercontinental missiles with a range of 4,600 miles. China has constructed two other Jin-class SSBNs that are being outfitted at Huludao Shipyard, Liaoning province. Four are in service.

Shang class (Type 093) nuclear-powered attack submarines (SSNs) are 110m long with an 11m-wide beam and can travel up to 30kts when submerged. Their weapons systems include torpedoes and cruise missiles. Six are in service.

Fishermen from nearby Vietnam claim China's building work and formation of artificial islands and reefs is destroying marine life in the region. (US DoD)

China has pledged to reunite Taiwan with the mainland – much to the anger of those in Taipei. (US DoD)

A Song class conventional powered submarine in service with the Peoples' Liberation Navy. (PLAN)

A Chinese Type 033 diesel electric submarine, which is based on the Soviet Romeo class. (PLAN)

a 9.9m-wide-beam and can travel at up to 20kts when submerged. The Project 636 vessels are 72.6m long and can travel up to 17kts when submerged. The Chinese Kilos have the capability to launch the Russian Novator 3M-54E Klub S cruise missile.

Song class (Type 039) diesel-electric attack submarines (SSKs) are 74.9m long with an 8.4m-wide beam and can travel up to 22kts when submerged. Their weapons systems include torpedoes and anti-ship missiles. Thirteen are in service.

Ming class (TYPE 035) diesel-electric attack submarines (SSKs) are 76m long with a 7.6m-wide beam and can travel up to 18kts when submerged. Many variants of Type 035 class submarines have been developed, such as Type 035G and Type 035B. All Ming-class submarines have 533mm torpedo tubes and Type 035B are capable of firing cruise missiles from its torpedo tubes. At least 11 are in operational service.

China's first submarine acquisition was on June 4, 1953, when the Soviet Union supplied them with 32 fully operational warships, as well as the licence to build the Soviet O3-class submarine. Since the mid-1990s, PLAN has purchased 12 Russian-built Kilo-class submarines, eight of which are capable of launching anti-ship cruise missiles (ASCMs). China is also expected to have received a Russian Amur-class submarine. ●

Yuan class (Type 039A OR TYPE 041) diesel-electric attack submarines (SSKs) are 77.6m long with an 8.4m-wide beam and can travel up to 20kts when submerged. Their weapons systems include torpedoes and anti-ship missiles. Seventeen are in service.

Kilo class (Type 877 AND 636) diesel-electric attack submarines (SSKs)

PLAN's Russian-origin Kilo-class submarines comprise two Project 877 vessels, two Project 636 vessels, and eight Project 636M vessels. The Project 877 vessels are 72.9m long with

Big nuclear-powered submarines are not always suitable for the shallow waters of the littoral. (UK MoD)

LITTORAL OPERATIONS

In the 21st century, operations in and around the littoral – the area of a nation's coastline – are seen as a potential key area for submarine activity. Here boats can sit and mount electronic surveillance on an adversary, launch a special forces assault or deploy a deception operation to confuse the enemy while the main attack takes place elsewhere.

In the post war years, diesel-powered submarines remained an important asset among western fleets. Then, with the advent of nuclear power, the US and UK focussed their resources on big submarines. The strategic thinking behind the change being that these new 'super subs' did not need to operate close to the shore (the littoral) and instead used their systems and weapons to overcome threats in these areas. Today, countries such as Iran use conventionally powered subs to trawl the waters of the Middle East and deploy even smaller midget boats to carry out reconnaissance in areas such as the

Persian Gulf. The constraint for small subs is that they can easily be located in shallow water, both from the air and by maritime surveillance. North Korea has invested in a fleet of Yono-class mini submarines, which are just 29m long and carry a crew of seven plus six special forces divers.

On March 26, 2010, the South Korean corvette ROKS *Cheonan* was attacked and sunk during planned anti-submarine exercises with the US Navy. It was alleged that the

Both the US and UK focussed their resources on big submarines. The strategic thinking behind the change being that these new 'super subs' did not need to operate close to the shore. (US DoD)

crew of the North Korean Yono mini sub had shadowed and fired a torpedo at the warship, killing 46 sailors. An international investigation concluded that this boat had likely sunk the *Cheonan* in a torpedo attack. However, North Korea vehemently denied the report's conclusions, and claimed it had nothing to do with the incident. The conventionally powered and so-called 'compact' mini submarines have remained a significant threat and are being adopted by an increasing number of nations who see them as cost effective and highly capable.

Conventional Submarines

Many fleets in Europe still operate diesel-powered boats, including Germany, Canada, Sweden, Norway, Greece and Italy. Further afield, China, Taiwan and Russia still maintain non-nuclear subs, while the Middle East, Pakistan, India, Bangladesh and Iran also field conventionally powered boats. Many analysts believe that advanced and heavily armed conventional submarines deliver greater capability in shallow waters compared to the much larger nuclear-powered boats. A smaller diesel-powered submarine operating in littoral waters, concealed by the ambient noise and seabed clutter, enjoys a significant detection advantage over a conventional submarine, according to some former submariners. The last conventionally powered boat to see operational service in the Royal Navy (RN) was the Oberon class. These 2,400 tonne boats, that carried a crew of 69, were built between 1957 and 1978, with a total of 27 commissioned into service

In the 1982 Falklands conflict, the RN sent a conventionally powered Oberon-class submarine HMS *Onyx* to the South Atlantic as part of the naval force which deployed to eject the Argentines from the islands. Buenos Aires also sent a conventionally powered ➲

Along the coastline, smaller diesel electric boats can sit and mount electronic surveillance, launch a special forces assault or deploy a deception operation. (NATO)

A North Korean mini submarine was captured by South Korea after it became entangled in fishing nets. (US DoD)

submarine, the Balao-class ARA *Santa Fe*. This had been procured from the United States and was used to land special forces at South Georgia, where she was subsequently attacked and later sunk by the Royal Navy.

In the late 1970s the UK Ministry of Defence proposed a diesel-electric submarine design to replace the Oberon class. This new class of submarine was intended to boost operations in the littoral. A total of four were built and entered service as the Upholder class in 1990. These 2,400 tonne boats – HMS *Upholder, Unseen, Ursula and Unicorn* – had a crew of 53 and, with their Paxman Valenta engines, could reach speeds up to 23kts when submerged. But in 1992, the UK government carried out a Defence Review and announced that the RN was to focus on nuclear-powered submarines. Thus in 1994, the Upholder class was declared surplus, and despite extensive appeals to retain them in service, they were eventually sold to Canada where they were renamed the Victoria class.

Conventionally powered submarines are much more cost-effective than nuclear boats. More and more nations are operating a new-generation of diesel-electric submarine known as Air Independent Propulsion (AIP). This system adopts marine technology which allows a non-nuclear submarine to operate without access to atmospheric oxygen and therefore surface much less than non-AIP subs. AIP technology has improved the stealth performance of a new generation of submarines at a fraction of the cost of a nuclear-powered boat. When operating on batteries, these subs are almost silent, with the only noise coming from the shaft bearings, propeller, and flow around the hull. This is a huge advantage over nuclear submarines which require large reduction gears and a robust cooling system to ➲

Many global fleets operate conventionally powered submarines which are cheaper to maintain than nuclear powered boats with smaller crews. (NATO)

Today, countries such as Iran use conventionally powered subs to trawl the waters of the Middle East and deploy even smaller midget boats to carry out reconnaissance in areas such as the Persian Gulf. (IRRG)

Smaller diesel-powered submarines, such as this Norwegian vessel operating in littoral waters, can hide in the ambient noise and seabed clutter. (NATO)

These 2,400 tonnes, Walrus-class boats have been in service since 1992, and the Dutch government is reviewing replacement options. Portugal maintains a small sub fleet of two Tridente-class boats which carry a crew of 33. These 1,700 tonne vessels operate a fuel cell AIP system and entered service in 2010. Their neighbour Spain currently operates one boat – a Galerna-class vessel which has been in service since 1983. The Spanish Navy has ordered four new S-80 Plus-class boats with AIP technology that are due to enter service in 2025. Turkey has a strong fleet of 12 vessels in service which include four Atilay class, built in the 1980s, that are still in service, as well as four Preveze class and four Gür class (Type 209 class). Ankara has ordered six Reis-class Type 214 submarines which will feature AIP systems. Turkey has a strong fleet of 12 vessels in service which include four Atilay class, built in the 1980s, as well as four Preveze class and four Gür class (Type 209 class). Ankara has ordered six Reis class Type 214

maintain safe operation of the reactor. Noisy pumps constantly circulate cooling water around the reactor core, then pump the same water back into the ocean, leaving nuclear submarines with a much larger infrared heat signature. In addition, improvements in battery technology have extended the range of AIP diesel submarines. With electro-catalytic fuel cells and the high energy density of lithium-ion batteries, AIP submarines can operate at a quiet state or rest on the seabed for several weeks without surfacing. This compares to the standard diesel-electric boats which must surface every few days. It is this ability, with AIP, to remain undetected that threatens nuclear boats which risk falling victim to a conventional attack. An example of an AIP sub is the German Type 212 class which can stay underwater without snorkelling for several weeks, travelling distances up to 1,500 miles or more.

The NATO alliance can field more than 100 submarines – many of them conventionally powered. Germany operates six Type 212 submarines which feature fuel cell and AIP technology. The Netherlands operates four diesel-electric powered hunter-killer subs for deep ocean and special forces operations.

Air Independent Propulsion-powered submarines can stay submerged for much longer than boats which rely on diesel-electric power and need to surface to recharge their batteries. (NATO)

The Egyptian Navy has operated both Russian Kilo class and German 209 vessels. (NATO)

The last conventionally powered boats to see operational service in the Royal Navy was the Oberon class which deployed to the Falklands and served in the Gulf War. (UK MoD)

submarines which will feature AIP systems. The first Reis-class submarine, Piri Reis, was launched at Gölcük Naval Shipyard on March 23, 2021 – the remainder are due to be commissioned by 2027.

The Italian Navy currently operates a submarine flotilla comprised of four improved Sauro-class vessels and four modern Type 212A Todaro-class units – these newer vessels are fitted with AIP. The Greek (Hellenic Navy) maintains a submarine force of 11 submarines. The newest and most advanced boat of the fleet is the Type 214 Papanikolis-class submarine. The Type 214 is a diesel-electric submarine developed by the German Howaldtswerke-Deutsche Werft (HDW) and is considered to be one of the most advanced conventional submarines in service. It features diesel propulsion and an additional AIP system using Siemens proton-exchange membrane fuel cells. The 11-strong fleet includes seven Type 209 Glavkos-class boats and a small number of upgraded 209s listed as Poseidon class.

The Buenos Aires Baiao-class ARA *Santa Fe* was used to land special forces at South Georgia where she was attacked and later sunk by the Royal Navy. (DPL)

The Upholder class submarine was ordered to replace the Oberon and boost operations in the littoral. (UK MoD)

Royal Marine Commandos on an Astute-class submarine prior to an assault into Norway during a NATO exercise. (UK MoD)

Air Independent Propulsion

Over the past two decades, technology has seen substantial increases in diesel engine efficiency, which has allowed AIP submarine commanders to further increase range and endurance. The aim of AIP is to produce oxygen within the submarine itself. There are two methods to produce large amounts of oxygen; one is the High-Test Peroxide (HTP),

which is concentrated hydrogen peroxide at 85 to 98%, while the other method is using stored liquid oxygen from cryogenic tanks. The most preferred designs are the Stirling engine and fuel cell.

The stealth advantage of AIP has been demonstrated in numerous naval manoeuvres and wargames. In 2005 during a NATO exercise when the Swedish AIP submarine HSwMS

Gotland 'sank' (on paper) two US Navy nuclear fast-attack subs as well as a destroyer and the aircraft carrier USS *Ronald Reagan* (CVN-76). While this was an exercise, the capability of the AIP sub prompted the US Navy to review the use of AIP. In a separate incident in 2001, a German Type 206 submarine breached the defences around the American aircraft carrier USS *Enterprise*, during another exercise, meaning

The Upholders were sold to Canada to replace the nuclear-powered Astute class which can sometimes be seen at Gibraltar on port visits. (David Parody/DPL)

While the Astute class is nuclear powered, the UK uses the submarines to support littoral operations with success. (UK MoD)

it was able to evade the nuclear submarines that escorted it. The U-24, German Type 206 diesel-electric submarine managed to evade *Enterprise*'s sonar shield and fired off green flares to show its position – which indicated that 'in exercise terms' the submarine had sunk the carrier. The incident prompted a review of tactics and a 'deep look' by the US Navy into the ability of conventional powered submarines. Just months before this incident, an Australian Collins-class submarine, HMAS *Waller*, which was taking part in naval exercises off Hawaii, was able to get so close to the Nimitz-class aircraft carrier USS *Abraham Lincoln* (CVN-72) that the command team were able to take photographs of the carrier through its periscope. The Australian sub managed to avoid detection from surface ships, as well as a Los Angeles-class nuclear-powered fast attack submarine.

Non-AIP conventional powered submarines rely on standard diesel-electric engines. They burn diesel fuel to generate mechanical power which on the surface is used to drive the submarine's propellers, which in turn move the submarine forward through the water. When the submarine needs to submerge, the crew shut off the diesel engines and source power from batteries to operate electric motors.

ARA San Juan

There are risks associated with all classes of submarine and in November 2017, the Argentine Navy reported a TR-1700-class submarine, named the ARA *San Juan*, missing. The incident is understood to have happened when the boat was on route to the Argentines

Having deployed the commandos, the submarine submerged in the Norwegian fjord. (UK MoD)

naval base in Mar del Plata. The submarine was officially listed as missing on November 15, 2017, with 44 crew onboard, as she undertook a routine patrol in the South Atlantic waters off Patagonia. She was believed to have suffered an electrical malfunction, and a multi-nation search operation was mounted. Within hours of *San Juan*'s last transmission, an acoustic anomaly consistent with an implosion was detected in the vicinity of the vessel's last known location. When the submarine was not located for a week, the crew were presumed dead by the Argentine government. On November 30, the search-and-rescue operation was abandoned.

The crushed wreckage was located almost exactly one year later, on November 16, 2018, by the Seabed Constructor, a ship owned by US search firm Ocean Infinity, after a long, traumatic search for submarine that drew attention from across the globe.

One of the most probable reasons for the disappearance of the German-made submarine remains an 'operational error'. The submarine's commander, Captain Pedro Fernández, said in a transmission to his superiors made in the early hours of November 15, 2017, that the vessel "was cruising at surface-level due to a short-circuit in the battery tanks, originating ➲

AIP technology has improved the stealth performance of a new generation of submarines at a fraction of the cost of a nuclear-powered boat. (NATO)

When operating on batteries, these AIP subs are almost silent, with the only noise coming from the shaft bearings, propeller, and flow around the hull. (US DoD)

believed the engines had not been shut down properly while the boat was submerged. In April 2021 the Indonesian sub, KRI *Nanggala*, a Cakra-class German-made Type 209 diesel-electric submarine disappeared in waters 51 miles north of Bali. The vessel had been involved in a torpedo firing exercise when it went missing. The Indonesian Navy, assisted by other countries, conducted a search, and a few days later found debris. It was later announced that the sub had imploded. All 53 crew members died in the incident.

Conventional Operators

Non-nuclear submarines can be hard to detect and are especially effective in water less than 100m deep where big boats find it hard to operate. This makes them less detectable

from a fire, most likely due to water entering the battery tank through the ventilation system". It is understood he then ordered the boat to submerge to 40m to repair the batteries and allow the crew to rest. An inquiry revealed that water may have flowed into the battery tanks of the submarine, generating a short-circuit in the battery tank. The fire could have generated increased levels of hydrogen which may have then ignited.

The loss of 44 crewmen constituted the largest loss of life aboard a submarine since the sinking of the Chinese Ming-class conventional submarine *Great Wall* (codenamed 361) in which all 70-crew died. In April 2003, during a military exercise in the Yellow Sea between North Korea and naval assets from China's Shandong Province, the vessel suffered a mechanical failure. According to the official Chinese news agency Xinhua, the crew members died when the submarine's diesel engines used up all available oxygen. It is

Sonar operators at work inside an Italian submarine during a NATO exercise. (NATO)

An Indian Navy Kalvari-class sub. These diesel-electric attack submarines were designed in France and built in India. (Indian MoD)

by passive sonar, blending more seamlessly into ambient marine noise. More agile and manoeuvrable compact submarines can navigate closer to the seabed and effectively use natural ocean clutter as camouflage, making them almost invisible to some sensors. In addition, midget submarines, such as the Iranian Ghadir boats and even smaller subs used by North Korea, present a challenge for warships and large submarines.

The Strait of Hormuz, between Iran and Oman, is an example of a location where midget submarines have an advantage. It has a depth ranging between 80ft and 120ft which is deep enough for warships but too shallow for nuclear submarines, many of which have a beam of more than 100ft and need to transit the Strait on the surface. As well as the shallow waters, the strong currents of the Strait both hamper and aid submarines. The sound of the

water provides a noisy background to help cover up the sound of a submarine. But from the air the shallow water makes it easier for reconnaissance aircraft to visually identify a submarine.

The Islamic Republic of Iran Navy commands a submarine force of 27 vessels, although exactly how many are fully serviceable is unknown. IRIN plays a crucial strategic role in the country's national defence due to its ➲

Modern nuclear submarine commanders claim diesel-electric subs, such as this Peruvian vessel, are easier to track because they need to surface regularly. (NATO)

dependence on the Persian Gulf for trade and security. As well as the Persian Gulf, Iran's naval forces operate in the Caspian Sea, the Gulf of Oman, the Arabian Sea, and the Indian Ocean. Between 1992 and 1996, Iran commissioned three Kilo-class boats from Russia, naming them the Tareq class. These diesel-electric subs allegedly cost Teheran $600m per boat. All three are all based at Bandar Abbas naval port in the Strait of Hormuz, where one of the submarines is always operational at any one time. Their capability in the Persian Gulf is, however, somewhat limited as Kilo-class boats require a depth of at least 150ft and can therefore only access about one third of the Gulf waters. In 2007, Iran began deployments of mini submarines, listed as the Ghadir class and Nahang class. The exact number of these vessels in service is unclear, although US intelligence suggests they have 14 mini submarines in service. As well as the obvious role of deploying divers for sabotage missions, these vessels are fitted with torpedo tubes. Iran is actively expanding and modernising its submarine fleet. Originally, none of Iran's submarines were capable of firing ballistic or

The Spanish Navy is upgrading its submarines and are moving to an AIP submarine fleet. (NATO)

NATO submarines from Greece and Italy pictured during a submarine warfare exercise. (NATO)

cruise missiles. In February 2019, Iran claimed it successfully test-fired a cruise missile from one of its Ghadir-class vessels and added that compact mini-submarines, the Tareq and the Fateh, have the same capability. Iran is also experimenting with submersibles, unmanned vessels, and other submarines.

In North Korea, Kim Jong Un and his administration promote the image of a strong powerful submarine force comprised of Sang-O and Romeo-class conventional submarines, however, many are old and there is little evidence of their operational capability. The Sang-O-class was introduced in 1991, produced at Bong Dao Bo Shipyards in Sinpo. In September 1991, a Sang-O-class submarine ran aground and was captured by the South Korean navy. The Romeo-class submarines include seven which were directly imported from China between 1973 and 1975, while the remainder were locally assembled with Chinese supplied parts between 1976 and 1995.

An example of an AIP sub is the German Type 212 class which can stay underwater without snorkelling for up to three weeks, traveling distances of up to 1,500 miles or more. (NATO)

Besides the fear of being hunted by another submarine, a commander must evade helicopters and fixed wing planes tasked to drop sonar buoys to identify any boats in the area. (NATO)

In 2019, North Korea revealed their first ballistic submarine which is believed to be a re-built and upgraded Soviet-era Romeo class. Kim Jong Un's commanders named the converted submarine the Gorae class. Despite being smaller and less capable than other ballistic missile submarines, it is still a regional threat to Japan, Guam and even Hawaii. This single Romeo submarine however, with its one tube, should be viewed as a test platform with only limited operational capability. On October 20, 2021, North Korea announced it had successfully made a test launch of a ballistic missile from its Gorae-class submarine off Sinpo. It was detected to have flown about 370 miles at an altitude of 37 miles before detonating. The launch of the missile is understood to have caused serious damage to the Gorae-class submarine which had to be towed back to port.

North Korea's test missile firing came after South Korea fired a ballistic missile from its Dosan Ahn Changho-class submarine

Aircrew load sonar units to an aircraft. These are dropped into the water and send a signal that operators aboard the aircraft can use to find submarines. (NATO)

in September 2021. South Korea possesses nine Chang Bogo-class submarines. These submarines are 120ft long and can reach 21.5kts when submerged. They can remain submerged for about 50 days without surfacing. South Korea also has seven Son Won-II-class diesel-electric submarines. The Son Won-II-class is a hybrid diesel-electric/fuel cell submarine with AIP technology. They can travel up to 20knts when submerged. Again, they can remain submerged for about 50 days without surfacing. Both classes are capable of firing torpedoes and anti-ship missiles. In addition, Seoul operates three Dosan Ahn Chang-ho-class diesel-electric submarines. This is a hybrid diesel-electric/fuel cell submarine with AIP technology. At 200ft these subs can travel at up to 20kts when submerged. They can only remain submerged for about 20 days without surfacing. Their weapons systems are capable of firing ballistic missiles, torpedoes and missiles. ●

A Royal Navy Merlin anti-submarine helicopter takes off. Its crew can drop sonar cartridges or a sonar 'dip' to seek submarines lurking in the area. (NATO)

SUBMARINE RESCUE

Submariners are a positive group of people who train for the worst-case scenario but rarely discuss it. Personnel serving in most navies must undergo training to ensure that they have the skills to escape a crippled submarine. Such training often involves rising through a water-filled tower to simulate exiting from a disabled boat at 100ft under the ocean. It is not for the faint hearted and takes place in the Submarine Escape Training Tank (SETT), part of a compulsory and much feared course that was compulsory within the Royal Navy (RN) until March 2009 when the Ministry of Defence ended pressurised escape training. Other nations continue to do it, however.

Being trapped under the ocean in a crippled boat is a nightmare scenario for anyone and while submarines are much safer in the 21st century, accidents can still happen. The loss of the Russian nuclear-powered submarine *Kursk* in 2000 with all 118 crew and the disappearance of the Argentine diesel-electric boat *San Juan* in 2017 are stark reminders. Today, the US and RN maintain dedicated teams that are on call to support the rescue of a stranded vessel. The RN's Submarine Parachute Assistance Group

Submariners taking part in an escape training exercise. (US DoD)

Submariners are a positive group of people who train for the worst-case scenario but rarely discuss it. (DPL)

(SPAG) provides a rescue support capability to submarine sinking incidents worldwide, available at short notice and works closely with NATO's Submarine Rescue System. In November 2017, the SPAG team was deployed to the South Atlantic to join HMS *Protector* in support of international search efforts for the missing Argentinian submarine *San Juan*.

Submarine Rescues

The first rescue is believed to have taken place in Scotland's Gare Loch in Argyll and Bute on January 29, 1917. HMS K13, a steam-propelled World War One sub sank during sea trials. She had 80 people on board – 53 crew, 14 shipbuilder employees, five sub-contractors, five Admiralty officials, a River Clyde pilot Joseph Duncan, plus Commander Francis Goodhart and engineering officer Lieutenant Leslie Rideal, both from her sister submarine K14 ship which was still under construction. By 2200hrs on the night of January 29, roughly ten hours after the *K13* went down, the first rescue vessel arrived. Divers were sent down at daybreak and managed to establish ➲

The Royal Navy Submarine School Submarine Escape Training Tank at Gosport, Hampshire. (UK MoD)

Trainees being put through their paces in the submarine escape tank. (UK MoD)

240ft of water. Twenty-six of the crew, located aft, drowned immediately. Salvage ships and navy divers responded quickly, and the following day began operations to rescue the surviving 32 crew members and one civilian from the forward sections of the boat. At 1130hrs on May 24, USS *Falcon* (ASR-2) lowered the newly developed McCann rescue chamber – a revised version of a diving bell invented by Commander Charles B. Momsen – and, over the next 13 hours, all 33 survivors were rescued from the stricken submarine. On September 13, after long and difficult salvage operations, *Squalus* was raised and towed into the Portsmouth Navy Yard. The boat was formally decommissioned on November 15, renamed *Sailfish* on February 9, 1940, and recommissioned in 1940 after an overhaul.

In April 1963, the USS *Thresher* (SSN-593), a nuclear-powered vessel, sank during deep-diving tests about 220 miles east of Cape Cod, Massachusetts. At the time she was accompanied by the submarine rescue ship Skylark. As *Thresher* began to dive, the Skylark picked up garbled messages reporting "minor difficulties" but then heard no more. An extensive underwater search later revealed the wreckage of the hull, broken into six sections at a depth of 8,400ft. *Thresher* became the first nuclear submarine lost at sea. All 129 aboard perished and their deaths were to prove a defining moment for the US Navy, resulting in a new and rigorous submarine safety initiative.

The loss of the *Thresher* also kick-started the development of deep submergence rescue vehicles (DSRVs), with the US Navy

The surface pool of the Royal Navy escape tank. (UK MoD)

communication with the survivors using Morse code tapped out on the hull. Later that afternoon, an airline was attached to the vessel, enabling the ballast tanks to be blown. By noon on January 31, the *K13*'s bows were brought above the surface and supported by a barge on either side. A hole was then cut in her, 57 hours after she sank. Forty-eight people were rescued and 32 died in the accident.

More than 20 years later, on the morning of May 23, 1939, the Sargo-class diesel-electric submarine USS *Squalus* began to flood while deployed on a routine test dive off the coast of Portsmouth, New Hampshire. The engine room filled with water through the main induction valve and sank in over

NATO carries out regular submarine rescue exercises. (NATO)

If a submarine is reported missing, military aircraft will fly to the area and drop marker buoys. (DPL)

instigating the Deep Submergence Systems Project (DSSP) in 1964. By the early 1970s, it had yielded two advanced and highly capable submersibles named *Mystic* and *Avalon*, which attained operational status in 1977 after extensive sea trials and formed the backbone of the US Navy's submarine rescue capability through to 2008 and later a specialist RN rescue capability.

Survival at sea

Submarine rescue is the process of locating a crippled sub sunk and its crew and bringing the survivors to safety. This may be done by recovering the vessel to the surface first, or by transferring the trapped personnel to a rescue bell or deep submerged vehicle to ensure their recovery. Submarine rescue may be done at pressures between ambient at depth and sea level atmospheric pressure, depending on the condition of the distressed vessel. Self-rescue of submarine personnel by buoyant free ascent at ambient pressure may be the only way to exit – pending water depth and conditions.

The first escape systems were based on breathing apparatus used in the mining industry which was a primitive form of oxygen rebreather. The system used in the first escape from a sunk submarine was the German Dräger breathing apparatus, used when the U3 submarine sank in 1911. Similar systems such as the Royal Navy's Davis Submerged Escape Apparatus (DSEA) were adopted by the Admiralty in 1929, while the Momsen lung was taken into service with the US Navy. In 1946 an investigation by the RN found that there was no difference in survival rate between using an escape apparatus and an unaided ascent, so the free ascent was officially adopted.

Free ascent required the submariner to keep an open airway throughout the ascent to avoid lung overpressure injury due to expansion with decreasing ambient pressure. In 1962 the US Navy adopted the Steinke hood, a hood with a transparent viewport attached to a life jacket, which allowed the user to rebreathe air trapped in the hood during the ascent. Free ascent and the Steinke hood were simple but provided no environmental protection once the submariner surfaced. The Russian Navy developed their own system but these too failed, as incidents on the Russian *Komsomolets* in April 1989 sadly highlighted.

Helicopters can also be flown forward to mark the area. (UK MoD)

Sometimes submarines can have minor scrapes like HMS *Talent*, which hit its fin in the deep ocean. Both British and US fleets enforce strict safety measures to avoid major accidents. (Ray Wergen/DPL)

The US Navy Monsen lung rescue equipment. (US DoD)

The then Soviet nuclear-powered submarine *Komsomolets* was submerged at a depth of 1,000ft off Norway when a fire broke out in an engineering compartment due to a short circuit. Propulsion was lost and electrical problems spread as cables burned. An emergency ballast tank blow was performed, and the submarine surfaced 11 minutes after the fire began. Distress calls were made, and most of the crew abandoned ship. While rescue aircraft dropped rafts, the high winds and sea conditions prevented the survivors using them. Many men had already died from hypothermia in the Barents Sea.

The RN also found that better 'sea protection' was needed after an incident involving the submarine HMS *Truculent*, a T-Class diesel electric boat. In January 1950, the sub collided with the *Divina*, a Swedish oil tanker, outside the Medway. The submarine sank rapidly – a report later concluded that the crew mounted their escape, with 57 being

An Italian rescue helicopter overhead a Norwegian submarine during a rescue exercise. (NATO)

Escape kits were issued to sailors and distributed throughout the submarine. (UD DoD)

The LR5 Submersible

The LR5 is one of a series of crewed submersibles that evolved in the 1980s. It was operated by the RN and designed to retrieve sailors from stranded submarines with the ability to rescue 16 personnel at a time. Only two crew members are needed to operate the LR5 in normal conditions, though three crew members are usually deployed – the pilot, the co-pilot, and the system operator. The LR5 can operate in a sea state of up to 15ft with a maximum safe operating depth of 6,200ft. Eight trips can be done with the LR5 before battery recharge is needed, which allows the submersible to save up to 120 sailors on one full charge of eight trips. The submersible is fitted with an integrated navigation and a tracking outfit. This integrates the surface and sub-sea navigation data. Britain volunteered the LR5 to help in the unsuccessful rescue of the crew of the *Kursk*.

The LR5 submersible was used by the RN from 1978 to 2009, since then it has been leased to support the Royal Australian Navy as the UK has access to the NATO rescue force. Every three years the alliance hosts a rescue exercise called Dynamic Monarch which alternates between warm and cold water. In 2024 it took place off Norway with ten participating nations – Canada, France, Germany, the Netherlands, Norway, Poland, Sweden, Turkey, the UK, and the US. During the ten-day evolutions, participating navies and personnel were briefed on the very latest in submarine rescue technology, operational strategies, and above all, were able to enhance international co-operation to respond efficiently when lives are at stake. Exercise planners developed complex scenarios to reflect real-world situations submariners might face. Teams engaged in co-ordinated efforts to rescue personnel trapped inside distressed submarines, testing their capabilities in communication, operational procedures, and emergency response times.

For the first time, state-of-the-art rescue ships from Norway, Sweden and Turkey joined the manoeuvres. Specialist equipment used included the NATO Submarine Rescue ➲

could carry 24 survivors and were made to be airlifted to a port near to the disabled submarine. The concept was to operate them from the deck of a suitable merchant vessel. Other navies followed this example and developed their own rescue solutions. The RN's LR5 Submarine Rescue Vehicle was also designed to operate from any surface vessel, such as a tug or support boat, which had a deck low to the water surface. After the *Kursk* submarine disaster in August 2000, when the Russian nuclear submarine exploded while submerged in the Barents Sea with the loss of 118 crew, the International Submarine Escape and Rescue Liaison Office (ISMERLO) was formed to help direct future rescues. The International Submarine Escape and Rescue Liaison Office (ISMERLO) was established by NATO in 2003 and aims to support and facilitate an international response to any submarine in distress.

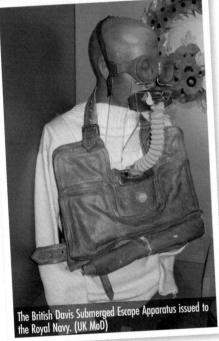

The British Davis Submerged Escape Apparatus issued to the Royal Navy. (UK MoD)

The Davis system being used in the Royal Navy dive tank at Gosport. (UK MoD)

swept away. A total of 15 survivors were picked up, but most died in the freezing water conditions. These incidents highlighted the need to protect survivors from the elements once they were on the surface. During the 1990s most of the world's navies using submarines replaced their escape systems with the British-developed Submarine Escape Immersion Equipment (SEIE). It was rated for escape from a depth of 450ft and covered the user completely, providing thermal protection and flotation.

Built-in escape pods have been investigated by the Russian Navy and were considered by the US Navy before they decided on a system of deep submergence rescue vehicles which entered service during the 1970s. These were small, crewed submarines which could be carried by another submarine and deployed underwater, making them largely unaffected by surface weather conditions. The initial models taken into service by the US Navy

The view looking down into the Royal Navy escape tank with a submariner wearing the new immersion suit. (UK MoD)

Members of the Submarine Parachute Assistance Group undergo the basic RAF Parachute Course at Brize Norton. (DPL)

System (NSRS), a rescue submersible that can evacuate submariners from a stricken vessel. Jointly owned by France, Norway, and the UK, it is based at the UK's naval base in Scotland. It can dive to around 1,800ft to dock with escape hatches, enabling those inside to get out. It can rescue up to 15 people at a time, including patients on stretchers, returning them to the surface. Operating teams aim to have it anywhere in the world within 96 hours.

Escape Training

A Submarine Escape Training Tower (SETT) is a facility used for training submariners in methods of emergency escape from a disabled boat underwater. It is a deep tank filled with water with at least one underwater entrance at depth, simulating an airlock in a submarine.

Since the 1930s, towers have been built for use by the RN, US Navy, Royal Australian Navy, and in several other countries. The SETT was a 100ft-deep specialist facility primarily operated to conduct training with submarine escape equipment, operated by the RN. The facility was located close to the Fleet's naval base at Portsmouth and featured a fresh, chlorinated water column with a single escape chamber – as fitted to some classes of RN submarines at the time. This allowed students to conduct a fully representative escape cycle from 100ft and closely replicating actions which would be required if forced to abandon a distressed submarine from depth. A dedicated boiler house maintained the tower's water temperature at 34°C. The SETT was commissioned in 1954, with the first students trained in July of that year. Since

then, completion of 'the Tank' has been a rite of passage for all RN Submariners. Ascents from increasing depths as well as lectures and practical training in how to survive within a disabled submarine, operation of emergency equipment and survival techniques on reaching the surface formed a package of potentially lifesaving skills. Over the years, as well as RN students, the SETT has been used to train submariners from Italy, USA, Greece, Canada, Israel, Russia, Venezuela, Turkey, Australia, and the Netherlands – with the staff and facility enjoying a worldwide reputation for excellence and good practice. Owing to a combination of increased safety associated with modern submarine design, submarines operating in areas where escape would be impossible with current equipment and the risks associated with the conduct of training, the RN discontinued pressurised submarine escape training in March 2009. The staff at SETT were drawn from the ranks of the UK Submarine Service. All members of SETT staff formed what was called the SMERAT (Submarine Escape and Rescue Advisory Team), as well as members from the UK Submarine Parachute Assistance Group (SPAG).

US Navy escape towers were known as Escape Training Tanks (ETT). From the 1930s through to the 1990s, they were used for training in buoyant ascent using the Momsen lung – a primitive underwater rebreather system used before and during World War Two by US submariners as emergency escape gear. After that, the Steinke hood was also regularly used. Inventor Lt Harris Steinke designed an inflatable life jacket with a hood that completely enclosed the wearer's head, trapping a bubble of breathable air. It was designed to assist buoyant ascent and was an advancement over

Pending the submarine's location, an RAF aircraft will fly a team from Submarine Parachute Assistance Group who will jump in and mark the areas. (UK MoD)

The Royal Navy's original LR5 rescue submersible. (UK MoD)

Submariners from across NATO forces exercise with a submersible rescue unit. (NATO)

A US Navy submarine rescue chamber which locks onto the submarine and allows the crew to escape. (US DoD)

the Momsen lung. Steinke invented and tested it in 1961 by escaping from the USS *Balao* at a depth of 318ft. It became standard equipment in all US submarines throughout the Cold War. The US Navy replaced Steinke hoods on US submarines with escape suits called Submarine Escape Immersion Equipment in the late 2000s. Similar 'escape towers' to train submariners are operated by the Royal Australian Navy in Norway, Sweden, and in Turkey. The German Navy operates a 118m-deep escape training

Every couple of years the Submarine Parachute Assistance Group mounts an exercise to validate their skills. (DPL)

The US Navy's Mystic — a Deep-Submergence Rescue Vehicle for operations in extreme depths. (US DoD)

Depending on the depth of the stricken sub, divers will be sent down to investigate. (US DoD)

pool, built in 1977 at a damage control training centre in Holstein. Since 2013 the Netherlands Navy have used their own tank, as have the South African Navy at Simonsberg.

Submarine Parachute Assistance Group

The RN Submarine Parachute Assistance Group (SPAG) is a specialist team that provides a rescue support capability to disabled subs across the globe at short notice. The SPAG was originally formed from staff of the Navy's Submarine Escape Training but has since moved to HMS *Raleigh* in Cornwall. The SPAG can be activated at six hours' notice, to fly to a submarine sinking incident, regardless of the vessel's operator. The team may work in conjunction with the NATO Submarine Rescue System. It is trained by the RAF's parachute school at Brize Norton and uses static-line steerable canopies. Exiting the aircraft at the rear ramp, they first deploy pallets which

A US Navy carrier and its air resources will be sent to the area of a missing US submarine. (US DoD)

An artist's rendering of USNS Navajo (T-ATS-6), a rescue and salvage ship and lead ship of her class, some of which are currently on order. (US DoD)

contain rigid inflatable boats, as well as food, medical and specialist supplies. This equipment allows the team to establish a floating reception package for submariners evacuating the sunken vessel, providing medical support.

NATO Submarine Rescue System

The NATO Submarine Rescue System (NSRS) is a tri-national project providing an international submarine rescue capability. It is primarily available to the partner nations of France, Norway, and the UK, but also to all NATO nations and to any submarine equipped with a suitable mating surface. The process of alert and call-out is based on receipt of a signal or message that a submarine is in difficulties. The intervention system, which is centred upon a remotely operated vehicle (ROV) will mobilise to the scene about 24 hours in advance of the full rescue system. Once on-site it will locate the submarine using the most recent navigational

The US Navy's submarine rescue unit is available to NATO's Submarine Rescue System. (NATO)

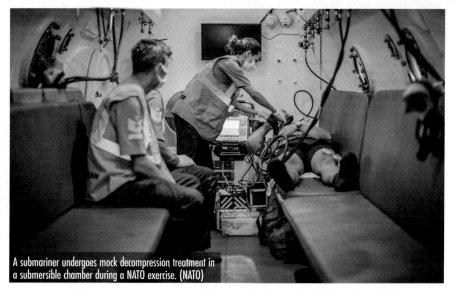
A submariner undergoes mock decompression treatment in a submersible chamber during a NATO exercise. (NATO)

positions reported. The NSRS will then support the submarine by establishing communications, conducting damage assessment, and preparing the distressed sub for rescue operations. The Submarine Rescue Vehicle (SRV), along with a portable launch and recovery system, support, and operating equipment, along with the treatment complex, should arrive on the scene approximately 24 hours later. All equipment and personnel will be flown to the mobilisation port for embarkation on a suitable mobilisation ship. The embarkation will take less than 18 hours, and the mobilisation ship will then sail to the scene where the SRV will be launched. The aim is to achieve rescue within 72 hours, with personnel being brought to the surface in groups of 12 to be transferred to the NSRS for treatment if necessary. The NSRS bases its ROV at the Royal Navy's submarine base in Scotland. ●

TIP OF THE SPEAR

Those serving in nuclear and diesel-electric submarines are in military parlance at the 'tip of the spear' with assets always deployed in defence of their nation. But it is the ballistic boats of the United States' Navy's Ohio class and British Vanguard submarines that are armed with Trident II, D5 submarine launched ballistic missiles (SLBMs), each with a potential range of 4,600 miles. They chillingly contain more firepower than all the bombs dropped in World War Two, including those on Hiroshima and Nagasaki. The French government has opted to use its M51 ballistic missile in its Triomphant-class submarine which also has an estimated range of 4,000 miles. The Trident missile can deliver 12 independently targeted warheads, giving each Royal Navy (RN) Vanguard-class submarine the capability to deploy 192 warheads. In practice it is the British Government's policy to deploy no more than 48 warheads per submarine in a combination of around 12 missiles per submarine, each with three to four warheads each. The devastating impact of these weapons has never been unleashed, but in an increasingly unstable world this deadly deterrent is maintained to protect against adversaries. It is at the centre of defence planning for both the US and UK and is regarded as the weapon of last resort. The decision to launch nuclear weapons can only be taken by the Prime Minister or a designated survivor following a nuclear attack, based on the instructions provided in the 'letter of last resort' (see Chapter 4). Two personnel must authenticate each stage of the firing process to avoid any errors. The firing control is not actually a 'red button' as many believe, but rather a trigger, modelled on the handgrip of a Colt 'Peacemaker' pistol.

Permanent Operations

Ballistic submarines are permanently on operations, always aiming to remain undetected and ready to strike at any time. Their presence alone sends the most powerful message to anyone who threatens the UK or the NATO alliance. They are rarely seen and receive little recognition for their work in their frontline 'unseen' operations. In addition to the ballistic

The ballistic boats of the US Ohio class and British Vanguard submarines are armed with Trident 2 D5 submarine launched ballistic missiles, each with a potential range of 4,600 miles. (US DoD)

boats, US, British and French sub-surface submarines (SSNs) lurk in the deep waters of the northern North Sea, the Atlantic, the Mediterranean and the Pacific, tracking, listening and monitoring Russian and Chinese vessels that will be at sea doing the same. The level of expertise among Moscow's and Beijing's boats has been questioned as they have often failed to identify a Western boat. Since the Global War on Terrorism began, Western submarines have played a key role in delivering a kinetic punch against enemies such as Al Qaeda and other terrorist organisations, launching Tomahawk cruise missiles at terrorist targets. While ground and aviation forces leave a footprint that can be seen and followed, a submarine can hide its acoustic signature and often operate without trace. These modern deep-water ghosts have improved propulsion systems and weapons systems which provide the ability to deliver impact out of all proportion to their size. The maritime environment has been and remains a testing domain where today's submariners use advanced technology to hide, hunt and harvest surveillance. In the 21st century their role is multifunctional, and they can mount a vast range of tasks, including anti-surface and anti-submarine warfare, intelligence gathering, mine reconnaissance, land attacks and defence of other fleet ships.

Ballistic boats

Ballistic missile submarines, often referred to as 'boomers' or 'bombers', carry nuclear weapons and are currently deployed by the US, Britain, France, Russia, China, and India. North Korea is also believed to have an experimental 'ballistic' submarine that is

Those serving in the submarine service are at the tip of the military spear – always on operations, although rarely seen. (UK MoD)

diesel-electric powered. The US Navy operates 14 Ohio-class sub surface ballistic nuclear submarines (SSBNs). These 18,900 tonne vessels originally carried up to 24 Submarine Launched Ballistic Missiles (SLBM) with multiple, independently targeted warheads. However, under provisions of the New Strategic Arms Reduction Treaty – an agreement between the US and Russia signed in 2010 – each submarine has had four of its missile tubes permanently deactivated and now carries a maximum of 20 missiles. The SSBN's new strategic weapon is the Trident II D5 missile, which provides increased range and accuracy over the now out-of-service Trident I C4 missile. SSBNs are specifically designed to mount extended deterrent patrols and with nuclear power, the only restriction to the length of a mission is the amount of food that can be stored aboard the boat. This can be huge, with a mixture of fresh and frozen produce ready to feed the crew for months. The US Navy's Ohio class submarines have three large-diameter

logistics hatches that allow sailors to rapidly 'store ship' with craned supply pallets, as well as allowing equipment and vital machinery components to be loaded quickly. The Ohio class is designed to be operated for 15 or more years between major refits and overhauls. After a deployment, a ballistic boat will undergo a minor maintenance period and routine safety checks before being declared 'fit' for operations.

The Ohio subs will be replaced with a new Columbia class, with the first due into service in 2028. A total of 12 submarines are planned, with the first two called *USS District of Columbia* and USS *Wisconsin*. The submarines will be 560ft long with a 43ft beam. The RN has four ballistic subs of the Vanguard class, also sometimes called V boats, and while the UK Government never discusses submarine operations, it is known that at any one time at least one boat is at sea. These 16,000 tonne boats are due to be replaced by a four new Dreadnought class in the 2030s at a cost of £31bn. The French also operate four vessels ⮑

An artist's drawing of a ballistic missile being launched from an Ohio class. (US DoD)

The Trident missile can, if required, be configured to deliver 12 independently targeted warheads, giving each Vanguard-class submarine the capability to deploy 192 warheads. (US DoD)

The Russian Navy maintains 16 nuclear-powered SSBNs as part of its strategic deterrent and is perhaps best known for its older generation of huge Typhoon and Delta class subs. Moscow's maintenance and operational readiness of submarines remains unclear and while it claims to have 16 operational ballistic boats in service, most senior analysts at NATO and in Western intelligence believe the true number is nearer ten or less. The newest ballistic vessel, the Borei class, which entered service in 2013, is packed with technology and state-of the-art weapons. To date, seven of the 24,000 tonne Borei boats are reported to be in service and another eight are in construction. Moscow has also deployed a new intercontinental ballistic missile capable of carrying nuclear warheads from one of its submarines. The 36ft long Bulava missile has been designed to be the backbone of Moscow's nuclear arsenal and has a range of more than

9,000 miles. The first test firing from the Typhoon class submarine *Dmitry Donskoy* took place in 2010 in the White Sea. A year later, on June 28, 2011, the Russian Navy fired a second Bulava missile, launched from the submarine *Yuriy Dolgorukiy*. Moscow claims to have used thermal technology in the new missile which the Kremlin claimed boosts the weapon's range to 9,000 miles. After the test missile firing, the *Yury Dolgorukiy*, joined the Russian Navy on January 10, 2013, and was actively deployed in 2014 after a series of operational test exercises. Moscow has converted some of its older ballistic submarines, mainly Delta and Akula class, into special capabilities vessels, capable of deploying as 'mother ships' for attached smaller 'deep dive' mini-subs. While unconfirmed, these converted subs can allegedly still carry ballistic weapons – although their serviceability has been questioned and none have been at sea for several years.

of the 14,000 tonne Triomphant class, the first having entered service in 1997. It was alleged in the French media that in February 2009, *Le Triomphant*, the oldest boat, collided with a Vanguard-class submarine, although the RN declined to comment on the alleged incident. Full scale development of the new French submarine, known as SNLE-3G (Sous-marin nucléaire lanceur d'engins – 3rd generation), was launched in February 2021. This new class, which has not yet been named, will replace the current Le Triomphant-class nuclear-powered ballistic missile submarines. The new submarine will benefit from an entirely new design and is reported to be almost 30ft longer, although the French Navy have not revealed any details of the new boat. The main driver for this increased size is new stealth technology. Outwardly the boat will include the X-form rudders and a pump jet propulsor similar to the new US Columbia and British Dreadnought classes.

Moscow's new ballistic submarines, the Borei class, carry the Bulava missile which has a range of 9,000 miles. (Russian MoD)

The SSBN Ohio class will be replaced by the new Columbia submarine in 2031. (US DoD)

The so-called 'nuclear trigger' which is used to fire the Trident D5. (US DoD)

The Bulava missile was introduced by Moscow in 2019 and deployed to the Borei-class submarine. (Russian MoD)

It is not just the US, France, Britain and Russia that operate ballistic submarines. China's ballistic submarine force is focussed on its six Jin-class Type 094 boats. According to the US Department of Defense, this is China's first credible sea-based nuclear deterrent. They were initially armed with 12 JL-2 SBLMs, each missile had one warhead with a range of 4,500 miles – capable of reaching parts of Alaska. By late 2022, they were rearmed with the JL-3 SBLMs which had the ability to strike the US. India is to build four nuclear-powered ballistic submarines with the first, INS *Arihant*, having entered service in 2016 and the second, UNS *Arighatt*, commissioned in 2024. These 6,000 tonne vessels are 300ft long and are said to have a submerged speed of 24kts. India will build two more ballistic boats by 2030.

The Trident Missile
The Trident II D5 is in service with the UK and US fleets. It is the latest generation of SLBM and is a major improvement on the earlier types, having replaced the ➲

The Borei submarines carry Moscow's nuclear deterrent and are understood to patrol the High North, in the Atlantic and the Pacific Ocean. (Russian MoD)

Submariners avoid dropping waste food in the High North as it quickly attracts unwanted attention. (US DoD)

Despite their social areas, like all submarines, Moscow's boats offer little room, with engineering spaces being very compact. (Russian MoD)

Russian submariners who serve on the Borei class are understood to have leisure areas they can spend time when off duty on long patrols. (Russian MoD)

Polaris, Poseidon, and Trident I C4 projects. Washington began developing the Trident D5 in March 1980. The first test launch took place in January 1987 and the first sea trial, which was unsuccessful, occurred in March 1989. The Trident D5 entered service in 1990. It was originally intended to significantly increase range compared to the first-generation Trident I C4. However, the Navy eventually shifted its emphasis from increasing range to improving accuracy. More accurate GPS systems have been tested on Trident missiles since 1993. In June 2002, the US Navy initiated the D5 Life Extension to replace ageing missile parts and extend missile life from 30 to 44 years. In January 2021, Vice Admiral Johnny Wolfe

US attack submarines spend much of their time hunting Russian boats to ensure they do not get close to either coastline of its mainland. (US DoD)

Britain's Vanguard class is among the most secret in the world with little known about its deployments or how long they last. (UK MoD)

announced the Navy would start the Trident D5 Extension Life II upgrade. The second life extension program seeks to increase the Trident D5's lifespan for another 60 years to deploy through to the 2080s. Since the Trident's design completion in 1989, the US has successfully conducted over 160 missile test launches. Today, the Trident II D5 SLBM is a three-stage, solid-fuel, inertially guided missile with a range of 4,000nm. The missile is launched by the pressure of expanding gas within the launch tube.

Attack submarines

An attack submarine or hunter-killer submarine is designed for the purpose of attacking and sinking other submarines and warships as well as conducting surveillance. NATO forces list these nuclear attack subs as Sub-Surface Nuclear (SSN) and diesel-electric boats as SSK – the SS indicating it is a submarine and the K that it is a hunter killer. In the Russian fleet attack subs are termed 'multi-purpose' submarines. Some attack subs are also armed with cruise missiles, increasing the scope of their potential missions to include land targets. An example being the launch by British and US attack submarines of Tomahawk cruise missiles into Afghanistan in 2001 following the terror incidents in America. Attack submarines can be nuclear powered or conventional diesel-electric – with many fleets turning towards Air Independent Propulsion (AIP) systems. They can deliver special forces, shadow a task force and spy on enemy forces, as well as providing protection for their own fleet's ballistic boats and making sure that adversaries do not stray into national waters or get to close to surface vessels. Attack or hunter-killer submarines in service with the US, British and French fleets are on average around 5-6,000 tonnes. They have the advantage over ballistic subs in that they can make port visits, with British SSNs being regular visitors to Gibraltar and bases in the Persian Gulf. Conventionally

US Navy helmsmen aboard a Los Angeles attack submarine. (US DoD)

The chef onboard a submarine has one of the most important jobs. (UK MoD)

powered submarines cannot compete with high speed of nuclear boats developed in the 1950s. The USS *Nautilus* was the world's first nuclear submarine and was operational in 1955; the Soviets followed three years later with their first Project 627 November class. The speed of the *Nautilus* was one of her main characteristics, allowing the submarine to harass surface ships and disappear before they could react. By late 1957, *Nautilus* had been at the centre of numerous US Navy exercises in which she was only located and 'killed' three times despite facing more than 2,000 so-called dummy attacks in two years. Using their active sonars, nuclear submarines could hold contact on diesel craft without risking counterattack as no-one could match their speed.

Sweden's AIP Technology

Sweden, now a NATO member, operates Gotland-class submarines which are ideally suited for the waters of the Baltic Sea – an area sometimes called the 'flooded meadow' due to its average depth of around 200ft. ➜

Officers navigate a Vanguard-class ballistic submarine into port. (UK MoD)

The US-developed Trident missile system is carried by both the Ohio- and Vanguard-class boats. (US DoD)

The Trident D5 missile is fired every few years in test exercises to make sure the system is fully operational. (US DoD)

The Russian intelligence gathering ship *Vishnya* watches a submarine-launched missile break the surface. (US DoD)

Gotland class, the batteries are saved for periods when the submarines need speed but otherwise cruise on the AIP. The subs can allegedly reach speeds of 11kts on the surface and 22kts submerged.

These submarines use liquid oxygen and diesel to heat the engine and cold seawater for cooling, which expands or contracts gases in the closed engine system which powers a piston to drive the sub's systems. Another advantage of the AIP system is that the submarines cost far less than a nuclear-powered sub but remain deadly quiet while cruising underwater at low speeds, even for weeks at a time. However, as well as the AIP, the Gotland boats are equipped with 27 electromagnets, strategically positioned to counter magnetic signatures that could expose their presence to enemy sensors. The technology is regarded as a 'genius invention' and particularly useful for countering magnetic-influenced mines. In addition, to reduce acoustic detection, the hulls of the Gotland-class submarines are coated with a secret sonar-resistant material that can absorb and scatter sound waves, making the submarines more challenging to detect for sonar operators and their systems.

Tomahawk Land Attack Missile

The Tomahawk Land Attack Missile (TLAM) is an all-weather, long range, subsonic cruise missile used for deep land attack warfare and can be launched from US and UK navy submarines. The Tomahawk Block IV (Tactical Tomahawk, TLAM-E), conventional variant, which entered service with the fleet in 2004, provides the capability to reprogram the missile while in-flight via two-way satellite

That makes it too shallow for the nuclear-powered submarines that comprise the bulk of Russia's submarine fleet and all of the US Navy's submarines. The Gotland-class hunter-killer submarines were the world's first diesel submarines to use an AIP system based on the Stirling engine. It operates a system in which heating and cooling gases in a closed circuit can be harnessed for motion. The AIP system, which is usually exclusive to nuclear-powered submarines, allows Stockholm's vessels to stay submerged for weeks. Most diesel engine submarines typically need to surface every few days or draw in air from the snorkel to recharge the batteries – an operation which can compromise their position. Instead, with the

The Tomahawk cruise missile has been fired numerous times in combat by US and UK subs. (US DoD)

The submarine often rises to periscope depth when it fires a missile. (US DoD)

capability. The first Block V missiles are from the existing Tomahawk Block IV inventory and have been re-certified and upgraded for fleet use. This mid-life recertification process replaces life-limited components in Block IV missiles to facilitate their remaining 15 years of service life and provides the opportunity for the missiles to receive modernisations.

Tomahawk cruise missiles are designed to fly at extremely low altitudes at high subsonic speeds and are piloted over an evasive route by several mission-tailored guidance systems. The missile has since been used successfully in other conflicts. In 1995 the US and UK signed a Foreign Military Sales Agreement for the acquisition of 65 missiles, marking the first sale of Tomahawk to a foreign country. In 2003, an agreement was approved for the UK to procure 65 Block IV Torpedo Tube Launch Tomahawks. ●

communications. This allows the missile to strike any of 15 pre-programmed alternate targets or redirect the missile to any new GPS target coordinates. The Block IV missile is capable of loitering over a target area in order to respond to emerging threats or, with its on-board camera, provide battle damage information to warfighting commanders.

Tomahawk missiles were fired from US and British submarine platforms during the 1991 Gulf War, Iraq in 1993, against Bosnian Serbs in 1995, then during NATO's operation against the Federal Republic of Yugoslavia in 1999. In 2001 Tomahawks were fired against targets inside Afghanistan, in Libya in 2014, in Yemen against Houthi rebel forces in 2016, in Syria in 2018 and from a US submarine in 2024 which targeted Houthis rebels again in Yemen. The US Navy received its first Block V configured Tomahawk missile from the defence contractor Raytheon in March 2021, paving the way to provide the fleet with an upgraded

The Swedish Gotland-class Air Independent Propulsion subs are regarded as the best conventional boats in the world. (Swedish Govt)

The Israeli Navy operates AIP submarines known as the Dakar class, which are built around German technology. (IDF)

FUTURE SUBMARINES

The United States has maintained its dominance in submarine warfare with advanced nuclear and ballistic boats. Since it launched the first nuclear-powered submarine USS *Nautilus* in the 1950s, Washington has continued to push the boundaries of sub-surface development to ensure that it will continue to protect America from future threats. Today, it is pushing the boundaries of new technology for its next-generation attack submarine, making it safer, smarter, and deadlier. The US Navy is augmenting its newest attack submarine fleet by increasing its capacity to deploy weapons and other key operational payloads for a potential conflict. Rear Admiral Jonathan Rucker, who headed the Virginia project, said: "The boats in this class are the most advanced attack submarines ever designed. Their stealth, firepower and manoeuvrability are superior to every other attack submarine force in the world."

The US Navy's new Columbia-class ballistic submarine. (US DoD)

The US Navy have adopted unmanned aerial platforms to assist in surveillance. (US DOD)

An Ohio-class ballistic submarine which will be gradually replaced by the new Columbia class. (US DoD)

At the same time, the US Navy is also developing an unmanned undersea vehicle project, the Manta Ray, which can operate at sea for months on top secret missions. The vessel has a diamond-shaped body and wing-shaped fins like a Manta Ray fish, hence the name. The aim is for this and other unmanned systems to operate ahead of the fleet's attack submarines in a reconnaissance and surveillance role – going into international waters and shallow areas undetected. Defence scientists are also working on projects to launch pods of small sub-sea drones from submarines which can launch deception attacks and harass enemy boats. The Royal Navy (RN) is developing an unmanned 17 tonne submarine which can be deployed from a frigate. In 2022 the RN ordered its first crewless submarine to shape future underwater warfare. Critically the vessel will be able to dive deeper than any other boat in the current submarine fleet with operations in the High North being an obvious advantage.

The Russians have also invested heavily in the future. President Putin announced more than a decade ago that he wanted to form a submarine force that was dedicated to 'Special Mission Capabilities'. Moscow's focus has been on developing small, manned submarines that have a 'deep dive' capability and can be carried under a mothership to an area of interest or operation. The Losharik special operations sub was launched in 2003 and at 1,600 tonnes was designed to sit in a cradle below an overhauled Delta-class sub. Other concepts included a remote sub that could be carried under a converted Oscar II. Both systems suffered setbacks and are understood to be awaiting further development; financial priority of the war in Ukraine has stalled funding for these projects in the near future. China and India are both reported to be studying future unmanned submarine plans, with Beijing seeking cost-effective options to mount undersea ➲

surveillance in the South China Sea and if needed, use remote controlled platforms – which can later be denied.

New submarines

The US Navy is building a new Sub Surface Ballistic Nuclear submarine (SSBNs) called the Columbia-class, which will replace the fleet's 14 ageing Ohio-class SSBNs. The Ohio-class submarines first entered service in 1981 and were designed to have a service life of 42 years – with a refuelling and major maintenance period. The new Columbia subs are scheduled to enter service in late 2031. The Pentagon identified the Columbia-class program as its priority project and ordered the first Columbia-class boat in 2021. Despite pressure on the defence budget, it is thought the Columbia-class program will remain funded even at the expense of other projects. The new submarine will be larger than the Ohio-class design in terms of submerged displacement and will therefore be the largest submarine ever built by the US. It will also be fitted with the most up-to-date capabilities

The Royal Navy's Trafalgar-class hunter-killer subs were replaced by the Astute class. (UK MoD)

Modern technology is replacing the periscope with a screen that delivers a 360° view of the ocean above. (UK MoD)

and stealth technology. The new 20,810 tonne Columbia submarines will be 560ft long, with a speed of 20kts-plus and be capable of diving to a depth of 800ft. These subs will be the most advanced ballistic vessels in the world. One of the most interesting design changes made to the Columbia-class is the switch to an X-Stern shaped configuration of rudder and propulsion planes, from the existing 'cross-shape' design seen on Ohio-class SSBNs and Virginia-class sub surface nuclear (SSN) boats.

The US Navy's Los Angeles SSN attack submarines are being replaced with the Virginia class. These boats were designed for a broad spectrum of open ocean and littoral missions, including anti-submarine warfare and intelligence gathering operations. The first Virginia-class subs have already entered service and the remainder will be acquired every year through to 2043 – they are scheduled

Unmanned technology is increasingly being used to protect warships and locate threatening submarines. (US DoD)

to remain in service until at least 2060, with later submarines expected to operate into the 2070s. A second class, the Seawolf, was originally intended to succeed the Los Angeles class, but high production costs resulted in the project being cancelled after only three submarines were produced. This setback occurred due to budgeting restraints at the end of the Cold War, and the decision to cancel the programme resulted in the final and third submarine being manufactured in 1995. At a cost of $3bn per unit, the Seawolf class was the most expensive SSN submarine produced for the navy. The Virginia class was put into full production due to it being smaller and more cost effective than the Seawolf. The class also has a large lock-in/lock-out chamber for divers. In Virginia-class SSNs, traditional periscopes have been supplanted by two photonics masts that host visible and infrared digital cameras atop telescoping arms. With the removal of the barrel periscopes, the ship's control room has been moved down one deck and away from the hull's curvature, affording it more room and an improved layout that provides the commanding officer with facilities that enhance his situational awareness.

Additionally, through the extensive use of modular construction, open architecture, and

The US Navy is developing a large unmanned underwater vehicle called the Manta Ray. (US DoD)

The Manta Ray will trawl the ocean seeking enemy submarines and their unmanned platforms. (US DoD)

commercial off-the-shelf components, the Virginia class is designed to be relevant for its entire operational life due to the introduction of new systems and payloads. Most of the changes are found in the bow where the traditional, air-backed sonar sphere has been replaced with a water-backed Large Aperture Bow (LAB) array which reduces acquisition and life-cycle costs while providing enhanced passive detection capabilities. The new bow also replaces the 12 individual Vertical Launch System (VLS) tubes with two 87in Virginia Payload Tubes (VPTs), each capable of launching six Tomahawk cruise missiles. The VPTs simplify construction, reduce acquisition costs, and provide for more payload flexibility than the smaller VLS tubes due to their added volume. ➲

Project Silent NEMO undergoes testing at Joint Expeditionary Base Little Creek. It is an experiment which explores the possible uses for a biomimetic application. (US DoD)

The Royal Navy procured their first unmanned submarine which is undergoing evaluation. (UK MoD)

Dreadnought Class

The UK government has announced the new Dreadnought class as the future replacement for the RN's Vanguard-class SSBNs. Like the so-called 'V Boats', they will be armed with the Trident II D-5 missile in their role of carrying Britain's nuclear deterrent. The Vanguard submarines entered service in the 1990s with an intended service life of 25 years and their replacement is a priority in maintaining the continuous at sea deterrent (CASD). The new subs were provisionally named 'Successor', being the successor to the Vanguard class. Then in 2016 it was officially announced that it would be known as the Dreadnought class, with the first of class being named HMS *Dreadnought*. The next three boats will be named HMS *Valiant*, HMS *Warspite* and HMS *King George VI*. The submarines will have a planned service life of around 35 to 40 years, an increase of around 50% over the previous class. They will each have three missile compartments containing four missile tubes (known as a 'Quad Pack') and five deck levels for a total of 12 missiles. Dreadnought-class submarines will also feature four torpedo tubes for Spearfish heavyweight medium-range torpedoes. They will be powered by a Rolls-Royce nuclear propulsion system known as the Pressurised Water Reactor 3 (PWR3). The MoD considered three PWR options, including the PWR2 system used in the Vanguard-class submarines, but the new design of the PWR3 adopts technology that delivers key benefits such as simplified operations, a longer service life and reduced maintenance costs over the lifecycle of the boats. The Dreadnought-class

Nations across NATO are developing unmanned underwater vehicles. (US DoD)

will be the first British submarines to feature X-rudders – as fitted to the US Columbia class. Previous submarines have used traditional rudders due to their speed and the depths at which they operate, improvements in control and safety now allow for X-form rudders. These new rudders will sit in front of the very latest pump jet propulsor and are designed to reduce the noise of the submarines, particularly at high speeds.

The Astute class is the new generation attack submarine that has entered service with the RN. Seven were ordered to replace the Trafalgar class – to date five have entered

service and two are still in construction. The subs have been named as HMS *Astute, Ambush, Artful, Audacious, Anson, Agamemnon,* and *Agincourt.* The UK project has suffered severe cost overruns and delays, with the cost of the first three boats increasing by 58% to £3.536bn and the fourth boat by 16% to £1.492bn. The Astute class has also been subject to a series of unfortunate incidents. In October 2010, HMS *Astute*, the first of class, ran aground off the Isle of Skye. In 2013 a crew member opened fire inside the sub, killing an officer. Then in 2016, HMS *Ambush* was in collision with a merchant ship, sustaining damage to her conning tower.

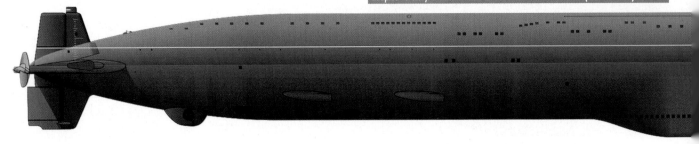
The Russian fleet have stretched a Yankee-class nuclear submarine which has been adapted to carry a remote manned submarine under its hull. (Russian MoD)

A US submersible undergoing an evaluation of its capability in the Mexican Gulf. (US DoD)

The RN has, since 2019, been investigating new naval concepts including 'fish shaped' torpedoes and submarine drones shaped like marine creatures to spearhead future underwater warfare. A whale-shaped 'mother ship' would be built from super-strong alloys and acrylics, with surfaces which can morph in shape, along with hybrid algae-electric cruising power and propulsion technologies, including tunnel drives which work in a similar way to a Dyson bladeless fan.

Russian Development

Russia is researching future capabilities including the use of artificial intelligence to generate avatar submarines that, working with unmanned vehicles, can attack a submarine force. Moscow's State Armament Program, which was announced in 2011, outlined plans to build and deliver up to 24 submarines – both nuclear and conventional – for delivery to the Russian Navy by 2024. Prior to 2012 there were an estimated ten nuclear submarine patrols a year mounted by the main Northern and Pacific Fleets. According to US intelligence, each lasted less than three months indicating a lack of operational readiness.

The first Borei-class ballistic missile submarine entered service in 2012, and Moscow's submarine activity quickly increased. The three Borei-class boats that were initially built included the *Yury Dolgorukiy* which was launched in April 2007. It began sea trials in June 2009 and was commissioned as a part of the Northern Fleet in late 2012. The second boat, *Aleksandr Nevski,* was scheduled to be delivered to the Pacific Fleet in 2012 as was the third, named *Vladimir Monomakh*. A fourth boat, *Knyaz Vladimir*, a modified Borei-A design (project 955A), was laid down in 2012. Six more units to this modified design were

subsequently ordered, the *Kynaz Oleg* and *Generalissimus Suvorov* being laid down in 2014 and launched in 2022. Two more in 2015 and 2016, and another two in 2021.

The mainstay of Russia's SSBN older force, the Delta IVs, joined the fleet between 1985 and 1991. As of the end of 2022, there are still six 'Delta' submarines in active service and an additional four under construction. Two further boats were planned to start conversion to 'special capabilities submarines' in 2023. The Kremlin's aim was to forge a fleet of huge 'mother ships' to operate in the dark deep waters of the High North and the Atlantic where these special mission boats could track and target seabed pipelines. The drain on Russian military budget caused by the war in Ukraine has put this development on hold for the time being.

In the Far East, a submarine arms race is intensifying as China embarks on production of a new generation of nuclear-armed submarines that will, in the next decade, pose a significant challenge to growing US and Western military capability in the Pacific and beyond. Analysts and regional defence attaches say evidence is mounting that China is on track to have its Type 096 ballistic missile submarine operational before the end of the decade. Beijing's new Type 096 SSBN is a largely an unknown quantity, but experts claim it will be more difficult for Western navies to track, boosting China's underwater nuclear capabilities. The Type 096 will be deployed in large numbers, delivering ➲

A Royal Navy nuclear-powered submarine is dwarfed by container ships as it enters port. (UK MoD)

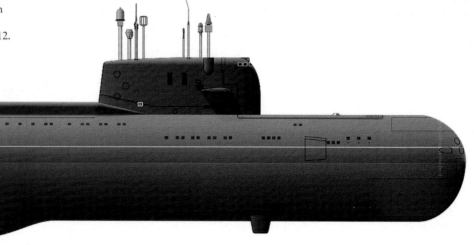

stealth, technology and expected to deploy over a wider area outside the Pacific.

AUKUS – Nuclear for Australia

In September 2021, political leaders of Australia, the UK, and the US announced the creation of an enhanced trilateral security partnership, dubbed AUKUS, to strengthen the ability of each government to support security and defence interests, building on longstanding and ongoing bilateral ties. The broader intent was aimed at Western influence in the Pacific Rim in response to China pushing its sub-surface fleet further south, claiming sovereignty of the South China Sea, threatening Taiwan, and seeking to dominate economic trade in the region.

Officially AUKUS will promote information and technology sharing and will foster deeper integration of security and defence-related science, technology, and supply chains. The project will boost Australian capability and intelligence co-operation between the so-called 'Five Eyes' – an intelligence alliance between Australia, Canada, New Zealand, UK, and the US. AUKUS will ensure Australia acquires nuclear-powered submarines – although they will not be armed with nuclear weapons. Beginning in 2023, Australian military and civilian personnel joined US and UK navies at bases in in both countries, to accelerate their training. The US plans to increase SSN port visits to Australia beginning from 2024, with Australian sailors serving alongside US crews for development training. As early as late 2026, the US and UK plan to begin forward rotations of SSNs to Australia to accelerate the training of Australian naval personnel. Starting in the early 2030s, pending Congressional approval, the

Modern submarines are covered in acoustic tiles to reduce their noise signature in the water – several are clearly missing on this vessel. (DPL)

Unmanned platforms can be used to provide a permanent sonar presence in areas where foreign submarines are suspected of operating. (US DoD)

A Wildcat helicopter makes an unusual transfer with a Royal Navy hunter-killer submarine. (UK MoD)

HMS Astute, the first of the new class, arrives at the Royal Navy base in Faslane, Scotland. (UK MoD)

US intends to sell Australia three Virginia-class submarines, with the potential option to sell up to two more if required. This will systematically grow Australia's sovereign SSN capability. Most importantly, it will require more deployments by UK and US nuclear submarines to Australia as the Canberra fleet trains to man their own boats in late 2030.

Climate Change

The climate change will have direct effects on future submarine operations. Increases in sea temperature, rising sea levels and a melting ice cap will all impact on a submarine's ability to operate and remain hidden. According to the Intergovernmental Panel on Climate Change, at current rates the planet will have warmed by more than 1.5°C between 2030 and 2052. Sea levels could rise by as much as 6ft and extreme weather events, with risks to marine and terrestrial ecosystems, will become routine. Changes in North Atlantic Ocean temperatures could lead to significant change in water flows. A change in ocean conditions in some areas of the world might change the

underwater sound landscape (soundscape) which could result in higher or lower ambient oceanic noise. At the same time, climate change could lead either to an increase or decrease in intensity of the acoustic signals radiated or reflected by submarines. The melting of Arctic Sea ice could expose the sea surface to winds,

which could change both ambient noise and acoustic propagation. This could force ballistic submarines to move away from the deep High North, where they are believed to patrol, and instead hide off the West Africa coast. Experts at NASA Space Systems, who study climate change, warn that oceans will become more ➲

Submariners aboard HMS *Astute* at Naval Station Norfolk, at Virginia on the East coast. (US DoD)

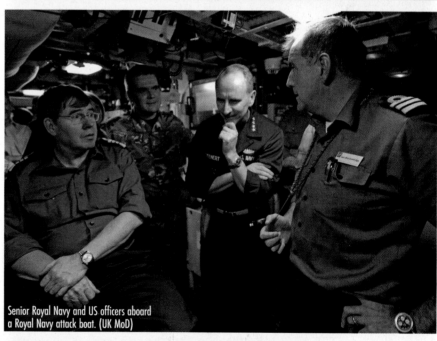
Senior Royal Navy and US officers aboard a Royal Navy attack boat. (UK MoD)

Swedish, American, and British companies are developing new and innovative underwater systems. (US DoD)

acidic due to higher concentrations of carbon dioxide at 1.5°C warming that will become even higher at 2°C degrees warming, negatively impacting a broad range of species, from algae to fish. Ocean oxygen levels will also decrease, leading to more 'dead zone' areas, where normal ocean waters are replaced by with low oxygen levels that will not support most aquatic life.

Unmanned Underwater Vehicles

Unmanned Underwater Vehicles (UUV) are at the centre of future naval strategy. The quest to invest in unmanned platforms is being driven by the requirement to reduce to human risk while at the same time cutting costs. This considers the ongoing recruitment challenges faced in the submarine service. Northrop Grumman's Manta Ray is seen as the future – but these are currently too small and basic to replace complex manned submarines, which require extensive crews to oversee the wide range of capabilities.

The aerospace industry has demonstrated how remote-controlled vehicles can replace planes and pilots as they reduce cost and risk. The MQ-9 Reaper is a remotely piloted drone that has been in service for more than a decade. Kamikaze drones like the Switchblade are extensively used in Ukraine. The F-16, a manned fighter jet, was recently successfully tested with a remote pilot. CEO of SpaceX Elon Musk has highlighted that the era of the fighter pilot is ending as the unmanned combat aerial vehicle, or drone, takes over. The question for Western naval commanders is could the era of the submariner follow a similar trajectory in the next 20 years? In

The Royal Navy's Astute class are reported to be fitted with some of the most advanced technology available, including touch screens in the operations room. (David Parody/DPL)

Future submarines will be able to deploy unmanned acoustic equipment and use drones to swarm and confuse an adversary. (US DoD)

Ukraine, war observers have noted the use of an unmanned surface vehicle known as a 'drone boat' to attack Russian warships of the Black Sea Fleet. Unmanned platform attacks reduce the risk of public backlash to political decisions which cost the lives of sailors. Humans require ongoing refresher training, salaries, housing, healthcare, not to mention pensions, so removing the human dynamic is cheaper in the long term. While much credit is allocated to using artificial intelligence in future warfare, it is unlikely that humans will be removed from the decision-making process. Drones can be calibrated to an algorithm and hence expected to perform in a consistent and predictable manner. Humans can import ethics, logic, and adapt to a changing environment and challenges – drones can adapt, but their decision-making process is limited. ●

The Royal Navy's future replacement for the Vanguard class which has been named as Dreadnought. (UK MoD)